Praise for *Beyond Ag*

"I highly recommend this book to anyone looking to enhance tice. Lucas's insights and expertise make this book a must-read for anyone seeking to improve their skills and knowledge in this critical area."

—Misty Kuamoo, VP, Security Shared Services, Nationwide

"Clarissa isn't blazing a path; she's paving a road for the early majority to reap the benefits of Auditing with Agility. . . . *Beyond Agile Auditing* not only provides the 'the why' but also provides an outline that prescribes 'the how' to succeed . . . I will share this work with all my champions so they too can begin to reap the benefits of Auditing with Agility to their organizations."

—Ray Ryjewski, Sr. Solution Engineer, HashiCorp

"In *Beyond Agile Auditing*, Clarissa Lucas's suggestions will provide auditors alignment with the business operations and deliver continuous value and risk response to audit stakeholders in real time. A must-read introspection for audit leaders."

—Yosef Levine, CPA, CITP, Partner, TechPar Group

"Clarissa Lucas' book *Beyond Agile Auditing* challenges the status quo and the conventional wisdom of internal auditing. She rightfully demands a mindset shift, suggesting internal auditors should collaborate with clients more effectively and more efficiently when rendering truly value adding outcomes. Her wealth of ideas can help practitioners to audit 'at the speed of risk' (as suggested by Richard Chambers and Norman Marks). "

—-Dr. Rainer Lenz, QIAL, CIA, CIIA, CEFA,
Chief Audit Executive at SAF-HOLLAND Group

"*Beyond Agile Auditing* provides a fresh, innovative, yet perfectly logical approach to auditing (with agility). I appreciate Clarissa's challenge to think differently, through her own stories of obstacles encountered and successes obtained. My curiosity is piqued, and I can't wait to try out some of these concepts. Thank you for offering a more flexible, collaborative, and value-driven viewpoint."

—Pam Pesta, Chief Audit Executive,
Erie Insurance

Beyond
Agile
Auditing

Beyond
Agile
Auditing

Clarissa Lucas
CIA, CISA, CIDA

Foreword by Misty Kuamoo

IT Revolution
Portland, Oregon

25 NW 23rd Pl, Suite 6314
Portland, OR 97210

First Edition
Printed in the United States of America

28 27 26 25 24 23   1 2 3 4 5 6 7 8 9 10

Cover and book design by Devon Smith/D.Smith Creative, LLC

Library of Congress Catalog-in-Publication Data
Names: Lucas, Clarissa, author.
Title: Beyond agile auditing : three core components to revolutionize your
internal audit practices / by Clarissa Lucas, CIA, CISA, CIDA ; foreword
by Misty Kuamoo, VP, Security Shared Services, Nationwide.
Description: First edition. | Portland, OR : IT Revolution, [2023] |
Includes bibliographical references.
Identifiers: LCCN 2022059549 (print) | LCCN 2022059550 (ebook) | ISBN
9781950508679 (paperback) | ISBN 9781950508686 (ebook) | ISBN
9781950508693 (pdf) | ISBN 9781950508709
Subjects: LCSH: Auditing, Internal. | Auditing. | Risk management.
Classification: LCC HF5668 .L83 2023 (print) | LCC HF5668 (ebook) | DDC
657/.458--dc23/eng/20230221
LC record available at https://lccn.loc.gov/2022059549
LC ebook record available at https://lccn.loc.gov/2022059550

ISBN: 9781950508679
eBook ISBN: 9781950508686
Web PDF ISBN: 9781950508693
Audio: 9781950508709

For information about special discounts for bulk purchases or for information
on booking authors for an event, please visit our website at www.ITRevolution.com.

BEYOND AGILE AUDITING

To Christian:

Keep chasing your dreams.

Contents

Part II: The Three Core Components of Auditing with Agility

Tables & Figures

Foreword

As an auditor, staying current on the latest techniques and methodologies is essential to ensure that your work is effective and efficient. As an audit client, Auditing with Agility can deepen your relationship with your auditors, produce higher-quality findings faster, and streamline your work management practices, resulting in less disruption to your team.

Clarissa Lucas has established herself as a thought leader and expert in Auditing with Agility. Lucas offers a fresh perspective on auditing in this book, bringing together real-world experience and research to provide a comprehensive guide for practitioners. The agile mindset is about adaptability and flexibility, and Lucas demonstrates how anyone looking for a new way of auditing can apply agility to their audit process.

One of the key benefits of the agile approach is the ability to respond quickly to change. In today's fast-paced risk environment, this is more important than ever. Auditing with Agility allows for continual learning and improvement, ensuring that audit results are delivered sooner, and risks are addressed faster.

Another advantage of Auditing with Agility is the focus on partnership, collaboration, and communication with the client. Traditional audit methodologies can often be siloed and disconnected from the rest of the organization. On the other hand, Auditing with Agility encourages collaboration and sharing of information, leading to a more holistic and comprehensive delivery of the common goal.

Lucas does an excellent job of highlighting the benefits of Auditing with Agility and explaining how to implement it in practice. She provides concrete examples and case studies to illustrate the concepts and best practices she discusses. This book is a valuable resource for anyone looking to stay up to date on the latest trends and techniques in auditing.

This book is for more than just auditors. The principles and practices of Auditing with Agility are relevant to anyone working in a rapidly changing environment. Whether in finance, technology, or another field, the three core components explained by Lucas can be applied to any process where you want to deliver value and results more efficiently to your organization.

I highly recommend this book to anyone looking to enhance their auditing practice. Lucas's insights and expertise make this book a must-read for anyone seeking to improve their skills and knowledge in this critical area.

—Misty Kuamoo,
VP, Security Shared Services, Nationwide

Introduction

Auditing is not always everyone's favorite activity, especially when you're the one being audited. Imagine this scenario. You lead a team responsible for a key business process or technology product. Your organization depends on this process or product for its survival. Perhaps your team is responsible for running the process that services customer accounts or for maintaining the technology product with which your organization's customers interact. Your organization is counting on your team's success to achieve its objectives.

It's a typical Monday, until your first afternoon meeting gets underway. In this meeting, you learn the internal auditors will be starting an audit of your process/ product in the next few weeks. You immediately break out in a cold sweat, panic and anxiety washing over you as your mind races. You wonder what questions the auditors will ask, what evidence they'll request, and what they'll report to their leaders.

You think, "The enforcers are here with their outdated checklists, looking for problems to shine a light on, wanting to make me look bad!"

The problem is, auditors don't understand your processes or what's really important to you and your team. How are you supposed to get your *actual* work done when the auditors are setting up a million meetings, endlessly asking irrelevant questions, and requesting documentation that doesn't even reflect the current process?

An audit adds work to your plate without bringing much value. Then, at the end of it all, they'll hand you a report that doesn't help you or your team deliver value any faster or better.

The auditors use the same approach they've been using to audit for years. Everyone else in the organization is changing to stay ahead of the change curve, but it seems like the auditors aren't even trying to keep up.

Now imagine yourself on the other side of the table. You're the internal auditor responsible for assuring the organization's key stakeholders that risks are managed appropriately and the organization is set up to achieve its objectives. It's a typical Monday for you as well.

In your first meeting after lunch, you explain to your client* that the Internal Audit department will begin an audit of the client's process/product soon. Before you even finish your sentence, the clients across the table cross their arms and exchange uneasy looks with one another, glancing nervously around the room. You can tell they're already getting defensive and shutting down.

"Here we go again," you think, trying not to roll your eyes. "We haven't even begun, and we're already off to a rough start."

You're only trying to help protect the organization that employs everyone in the room, but the people on the other side of the table already see you as an adversary. Don't they understand that your job is to help them? That the purpose of Internal Audit is to *help* deliver value and *improve* processes?

You try to change the attitude in the room by asking about the team's current process. After all, as an auditor, you're an expert in risks and controls, not an expert in every business process at your organization. You can't do your job effectively if the team doesn't help explain what they do and why they do it. However, instead of engaging in the conversation, the clients clam up and give you the most basic answers to your questions without elaborating. It feels like they're purposefully trying to hide information or obstruct your audit. It's clear they want you to be done . . . or at least gone.

And, when it comes to setting up time to meet with you, the team says they're too busy. You barely get a regular fifteen-minute meeting on the books before they're out the door.

Don't they care about risks and what could go wrong? The success or failure of the organization affects everyone, after all. They seem to be more focused on inventing the next new product or delivering the coolest new feature, when they should care about a strong control environment!

This scenario might feel overly simplistic, but time and time again this is the adversarial, even combative, nature of many internal audits. It often seems that both sides (auditors and those being audited) are bracing themselves for the worst. There has to be a way these two groups can work together, right? Or are we des-

---

* The terms "client" and "management" are used interchangeably throughout this book. Both terms refer to individuals or teams who work with auditors and are accountable for processes or products (e.g., technology, business products, services offered to end customers) that are reviewed by audit functions, such as internal audit, external audit, and internal risk assurance functions. The "client" in this book refers to both individual contributors and people leaders. Basically, "management" and "client" refer to anyone who is not an auditor or other assurance provider.

tined to be lifelong adversaries? How did we end up in this horrifying nightmare in the first place?

From Adversaries to Partners

For nonauditors reading this book, especially those in the technology sector, this scenario might look very similar to another example of organizational adversaries: software developers versus operations teams. For years, software developers and operations teams were at odds. They were not incentivized to work together. There was a proverbial wall built up between the two organizations, as has famously been illustrated.

The developers would write the code and then throw it over the wall to the operations team, who then had to deal with operating that code without knowing how and why the code was written in the first place. Developers were incentivized by the business to deploy "features and changes into production as quickly as possible,"[1] while operations teams were charged with "providing customers with IT service that is stable, reliable, and secure, making it difficult or even impossible for anyone to introduce production changes that could jeopardize production."[2] These two silos were routinely in conflict, resulting in slow delivery of value, low quality of code, and a lot of unhappy people.

Throughout the past decade, a new way of working called DevOps* has brought these two roles together. They learned that by working as a single team with a common goal, they could deliver value sooner, safer, and happier.

I'm simplifying here. There are many excellent books, presentations, and articles written on the success of DevOps, and we'll discuss DevOps a bit more in Chapter 2. What I want you to take away from this brief description is the idea that adversaries don't have to remain adversaries. There is a better way of working.

Let's think back to the scenario presented at the beginning of this introduction. Once again, we have two teams separated by a proverbial wall (or table). They are both working for the same organization, so shouldn't they be on the same side? Shouldn't they be working together instead of against each other? How did we get here?

In short, it's because the world around us has changed and, notably, the way organizations deliver value to customers has changed, but the way we conduct audits hasn't kept up with the change curve. Auditors perform their work using

---

* In the most basic definition, DevOps is an operating model where development teams and operations teams in a technology organization combine to become one team working toward a collective goal of delivering value to customers.

the same approach that has been around for decades. While this way of auditing has historically been successful, the current environment and landscape have changed drastically over the past few years. Furthermore, auditors apply that same approach in every situation, without accounting for unique attributes of a process, product, or situation that may drive the need for a different approach.

Auditors using the same way of working from decades ago without adapting to today's dynamic environment will find themselves pitted *against* their clients rather than working *with* them. The result is the adversarial scenario presented earlier.

If you're reading this book, you've likely experienced this. I know I have. While I've spent most of my career as an auditor, I have also been on "the other side of the table." I have been part of a team being audited. I can testify that being audited wasn't my favorite experience by any stretch of the imagination. From my time as an auditor, I can tell you that it isn't any fun for the auditors when clients see us as the bad guy or the antagonist.

Regardless of whether you're an auditor or someone who works with auditors, I'm here to tell you that you aren't doomed to be adversaries forever. There is a better way—a way for auditors and their clients to work together toward a shared goal. A way to audit with more agility, without slowing your team down, without the headaches and the hair pulling. A way for us to see one another as teammates instead of adversaries on the battlefield and to add more business value together. A way to get more value out of an audit. A way to help the organization deliver better value, sooner, safer, and happier.

A New Way of Auditing

We can all agree that we want a less painful and more valuable audit experience. Despite the barriers we all know exist, the real problem is seeing the audit process as it always has been rather than as it should be. Yet we can agree that change is inevitable. We need to modify our mindset and approach to get more value from an audit and create a better audit experience.

Imagine what that better audit experience looks like:

- Auditors and their clients work together toward a shared outcome and common goal.
- Auditors help their clients see risks, both those present today and those coming up on the horizon or around the corner.
- The client proactively reaches out to auditors for help addressing risk before it's too late and manifests into actual losses.

- Auditors' questions and requests are addressed sooner.
- Auditors are more efficient with their client's time and help their clients find ways to increase efficiency.
- Instead of the auditors getting in their clients' way, and clients getting in the auditors' way, the two groups help each other achieve a common objective, all while preserving the auditors' independence.
- Auditors not only remain relevant to their organization, they become essential to the organization's success.
- Finally, imagine both auditors and audit clients having fun during the audits.

Luckily, you won't have to rely on imagining this scenario much longer. You *can* work together toward a *shared* goal, and you can do it today. You need to look beyond what your relationship is and think forward to what it could be in the future . . . and be willing to radically change your way of thinking and working through an audit.

Some organizations have taken steps toward improving the audit process through incorporating "Agile Auditing." This has been a huge step in the right direction, but it hasn't come without its faults and downfalls. In auditing, as in the software community, Agile has been conflated with a strict set of practices that every organization, despite their unique culture and needs, must adhere to.

This doesn't sound very agile to me. This strict adherence to the idea that you can simply follow steps 1, 2, and 3 and suddenly be a high-performing agile organization has led to an inability to truly become agile and failed attempts at greater value through agility. As a result, many organizations have experienced slower time to value, unhappy employees, and lower quality products . . . or at the very least, a shiny new label on the same old behaviors and outcomes.

Agile Auditing, I fear, is headed in the same direction. Too many organizations see it as a quick fix: an easy framework they can implement to suddenly disintegrate the adversarial audit experience and ring in a new era of Agile Auditing.

Internal Audit cannot stop here. Strict adherence to a rigid, one-size-fits-all Agile Auditing framework isn't getting us to the promised agility, speed, quality, and happiness we need. We need to continue to push for more improvements. We need to go *beyond* Agile Auditing and approach internal audits with an agile mindset, not an Agile checklist.

Auditing with Agility, as I like to call it, is far different from the strict framework-focused world of Agile Auditing. Instead of trying to fit everyone in an organization in a single process, it teaches auditors a way of working that focuses on a **value-driven**, **integrated**, **adaptable** approach to the internal audit. Let's take a look at each of these three core components.

- **Value-driven:** In a value-driven audit, the scope of work is driven by what adds the most value to the organization. Each organization and team may define value differently, but generally, it could be areas of greatest risk or greatest opportunity for the organization. Value-driven auditors determine the audit's focus by leveraging the expertise and perspective of the team being audited. Internal Audit is not looking to hand down edicts. We are here to help the organization deliver value.
- **Integrated:** An integrated audit aligns the audit work with the client's daily work and integrates continuous improvement into the audit process. For you auditors out there, think of this as "Integrated Auditing* 2.0." The first version of integrated auditing was integrating the technology audit work with the operational or financial audit work rather than performing that work in silos or in separate audits. This book takes that concept a step further by integrating audit work into the client's daily work. The audit should be something the client participates in and happens *with* them rather than something that happens to them.
- **Adaptable:** In the context of this book, adaptable auditing focuses on improving the audit team's ability to respond to change and add flexibility into the audit process. It is a mindset and a way of working rather than a framework to implement. This element of adaptability is essential in today's world of rapid change, where organizations need to react with speed to survive. Internal Audit can't be the blocker to change; rather, they must learn to adapt with change.

Implementing these three core components results in a better audit experience for everyone involved (for the client, the auditors, and the organization). It moves teams from an audit framework focused on *outputs* to an *outcome*-driven approach.

An *output* is what is produced. Examples of audit outputs include audit observations and an audit report. While observations and audit reports are important, alone they don't help the organization achieve its objectives.

---

* Integrated Auditing 1.0 is a practice that integrates technology, financial, and operational auditing into a single audit. Historically, these types of audits were performed separately and either reported separately or pieced together at the end of the audit.

Outcomes, on the other hand, truly bring us closer to success. Outcomes are the "why" behind the actions, the expected improvements, or the measures of success. Examples of audit *outcomes* include better alignment of audit activities with emerging risks or greatest risks, stronger relationships and increased collaboration between auditors and audit clients, expedited delivery of more valuable results, and elevated awareness of and ability to address risk exposures.

Chapter 3 explores the possible outcomes of Auditing with Agility in detail. Then Chapters 5 through 7 discuss practices you can perform to achieve the possible outcomes.

Although this may all sound daunting, moving toward a practice of Auditing with Agility is worth the investment. This isn't just a dream or fairytale. There are organizations today, such Walmart, Barclays, and Capital One, that are working toward this goal right now . . . and succeeding.

In my own experience with Auditing with Agility, my clients and I experienced delivery of results sooner, fewer surprises (audit work became planned work for my clients), and more engagement from both auditors and clients (we had *fun* during the audit!). Another organization you'll read about later on experienced shorter audit cycles and more timely delivery of results through Auditing with Agility.

Another topic prevalent in discussions about Internal Audit's evolution in today's digital world is the use of artificial intelligence (AI) and machine learning (ML). AI is the use of technology to perform tasks that have historically required human cognitive thought. ML is a type of AI where the technology adapts its knowledge or "learns" based on additional data. Leveraging these advances in internal audit strategy and execution can increase the audit organization's effectiveness and efficiency. For example, teams leveraging AI and ML to evaluate risks can target their efforts in areas where the organization is currently at greater risk or is *anticipated* to experience greater risk.

While these tools can yield many incredible benefits, AI, ML, and specific tools are *not* the focus of this book. This book focuses on practices and process enhancements. Once those core elements are in place, then audit organizations can determine which tools can further assist in their evolution.

Not Just a Book for Auditors

It's tempting to think that this book is just for those in the audit profession, but this book is also for anyone who works with auditors or is subject to audits and yearns for a better experience. Change cannot come solely from one side of the table. If only developers had read books on DevOps, the practice would never have taken off. Both developers and operations teams needed to embrace DevOps for it to be successful. This book is for those on both sides of the table. For the auditors reading this book, this isn't just for IT auditors. It's for IT auditors and non-IT auditors alike. Both will find incredible value waiting for them in this book.

This book is for auditors who want to revolutionize their way of working to become strategic differentiators and increase the value they bring to the organization.

It's for teams who want to improve their relationships with their auditors.

It's for auditors who are fed up with common labels and stereotypes placed on those in this profession.

It's for audit clients who are at their wits' end with the current audit experience, who need to get more value from the time they invest with their auditors.

It's for auditors who, instead of going stagnant, want to keep up with today's pace of change, who are unwilling to let the profession's value proposition become a thing of the past. For the business executives who want to gain the edge over their competitors and who don't want to make headlines for the wrong reasons.

It's for anyone who wants to help their organization continuously improve ways of working, leading to better outcomes, and those who want to understand how auditors can help along that journey.

The primary audience for this book is those who work at large, complex organizations, as my personal experience and the personal examples I share are from my time at larger organizations. But readers at smaller organizations will also benefit from the concepts in this book, as they will find case studies throughout from smaller organizations as well.

Also, while the term "auditor" and "audit" are used throughout this book, the audience is not limited to Internal Audit functions. Other risk-assurance functions, like external auditors and internal risk management/assurance functions, can also adopt the concepts within this book and reap the many benefits.

How to Use This Book

Here's what awaits you inside this book. In Part I, I walk you through the past, present, and future of internal auditing. We explore the challenges organizations face when leveraging the traditional approach to audits. This first section of the book also explores how the profession has responded to the need to change the audit process by moving to Agile Auditing and the limitations and faults of this framework. It will also showcase my personal journey from traditional auditing to Agile Auditing and finally to Auditing with Agility.

Next, we tackle challenges commonly faced by auditors, as well as those faced by the auditors' clients (herein referred to as "clients" or "management"). Potential solutions to these challenges are also introduced in this section. We then introduce the benefits you can achieve through Auditing with Agility. From there, you will discover why organizations need to keep moving forward, *beyond* Agile Auditing.

Part II of the book gives you the tools to adopt the culture and mindset of Auditing with Agility into your practices and processes. It dives deeper into each of the three core components of Auditing with Agility: value-driven, integrated, adaptable.

Finally, in Part III, I leave you with tips on how to set yourself up for a successful evolution to better audit experiences—for both auditors and clients.

You may choose to start at the beginning of the book and read through it in order until reaching the end. If you seek a broad perspective from both the auditor's and the client's viewpoint, as well as a thorough understanding of each of the topics presented in this book, then reading cover-to-cover may be a good starting point.

If, however, you have a strong foundational understanding of traditional auditing practices, I invite you to skip around to the areas of most interest to you. Perhaps you are a client and have specific challenges with your auditors. Feel free to dive straight into Chapter 4, where we explore problems and solutions, for an introduction to the solution for the problem you're facing. From there, you may want to move to Part II to gain a deeper understanding of the specific practices you can implement to overcome those challenges. Or maybe you've tried implementing some of these practices and haven't been as successful as you'd hoped. If this is the case, you might want to skip ahead to Part III to troubleshoot your situation and find a better way to go about making the transition.

If you've successfully implemented Agile Auditing at your organization, select a new practice to experiment with. Take the next step beyond Agile Auditing to even more effectiveness and efficiency.

Better yet, perhaps you've successfully implemented Auditing with Agility in your organization. If you have, then you know that one of the key Agile principles is to identify ways to improve or to increase your effectiveness and then take action to do so. If this is your reality, I encourage you to jump to a section of the book with a title that seems a bit unfamiliar to you. There, you'll find new concepts and practices waiting for you to experiment with to further increase your effectiveness.

This book focuses primarily on improving the audit engagement itself. As an added benefit, it also explores opportunities to add value by applying better ways of working to the audit risk assessment and development of the overall audit plan—how audits are prioritized and scheduled each year. The primary focus though is improving the audit engagement itself.

We're all at unique points in our Auditing with Agility journey. As such, this book is intended to be revisited regularly as you progress on your journey and look to learn more, or as you encounter new challenges.

There are a large number of concepts introduced and explored in this book. I caution against taking an all-or-nothing approach and incorporating all of these activities at once. Doing so will likely result in an overwhelmed team, confused clients, inefficient audit work, and the eventual abandonment of better ways of working and a retreat to less effective practices.

Instead, select one or two concepts to experiment with on a single audit. Staff the audit with people who are excited to try something new and are open to a test-and-learn environment. Create a safe environment for them to try out these concepts. When things don't go as planned (it's not a matter of *if*, it's a matter of *when*), resist the urge to point fingers, place blame, and revert to old ways of working. Instead, empower the team to learn from their experiences and try again.

Speaking of a journey, case studies of organizations that are on their own journey to implementing Auditing with Agility are sprinkled throughout this book. The experiences, failures, challenges, and successes in these examples show how any organization can take on this transformation. It isn't a framework, it's a mindset change, a cultural change, and these stories show you exactly how it can happen.

The Past, Present, and Future of Internal Audit

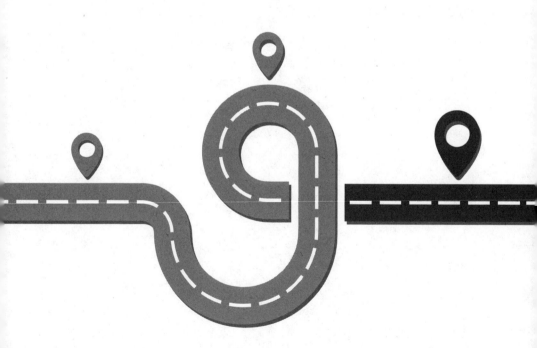

Chapter 1

The Legacy of Internal Audit

As I hinted at in the introduction, the legacy of Internal Audit in many organizations isn't exactly the most beloved. I think for the majority of those on the other side of the table, the word auditor brings about visions of cold, aloof, suit-clad individuals carrying clipboards and red pens and leering disapprovingly down at you. The epitome of red tape and bureaucracy, auditors are often portrayed as emotionless automatons dedicated to making your life . . . well, unpleasant.

In reality, Internal Audit can be, and is intended to be, a partner to your team instead of an adversary. The next time you hear that the auditors are coming, I hope you'll envision something closer to the smiling, supportive face of a coach or teacher, someone who is coming to help you instead of hinder you. Even more than that, a welcome addition to your team.

To help change this vision of Internal Audit, let's take a minute to dive into the value proposition of audit. I think it's fair to say that at some point, nearly all nonauditors (and even some auditors) have asked this very question: What is the real purpose of Internal Audit, and what value do auditors bring?

What Is Internal Audit?

Okay, instead of relying on preconceived notions about what internal auditing is, let's look at the reigning authority's definition of internal auditing. The IIA, or the Institute of Internal Auditors, and its affiliates set the standards for internal auditors globally.* According to them,

> internal auditing is an **independent, objective assurance and consulting** activity designed to **add value** and **improve** [emphasis added] an

---

* These standards have also been adopted by international affiliates of the IIA, such as the Chartered Institute of Internal Auditors in the UK and Ireland, as well as others across the globe. For more information on the IIA and its affiliates, visit https://www.theiia.org/en/about-us/chapters-and-affiliates/.

organization's operations. It helps an organization accomplish its objectives by using a systematic, disciplined approach to evaluate and improve the effectiveness of risk management, control, and governance processes.

Performed by professionals with an in-depth understanding of the business culture, systems, and processes, the internal audit activity provides assurance that internal controls in place are adequate to mitigate the risks, governance processes are effective and efficient, and organizational goals and objectives are met.[1]

Let's break that definition down a bit more. Look at the first sentence. "Internal auditing is an **independent**, **objective assurance and consulting** activity designed to **add value** and **improve** an organization's operations." The intention of every internal audit team is to be independent and objective, free from the natural biases that come from being immersed on a team or in a system or under the control of those accountable for the team or process (e.g., typically audit clients). In other words, auditors come to bring a fresh perspective, and fresh perspectives are essential in helping any of us get out of the muck. Who hasn't been so deep in a project that you can no longer see the forest for the trees (excuse the tired metaphor, but it holds true)? Audit is here to help. I know, I know; many people have modified Ronald Reagan's quote about the government being here to help to read something like this: "The most terrifying words in the English language are: I'm from Internal Audit and I'm here to help."

In reality, auditors truly are here to help. We want the organization to succeed just as much as the nonauditors do.

The second part of the IIA's definition of Internal Audit that I want to highlight is "consulting." Audit is meant to consult with you and your team, not to manage, dictate, or in any way create a bureaucratic mess. We're here to consult, to assist, to help.

Finally, the last part of that definition is possibly the most important. The purpose of Internal Audit is to "add value" and "improve" the organization's operations. Despite what so many might think, Internal Audit is not here to make life difficult or to add more rules. We want what you want: to add value and improve the organization. The only way we can both achieve our purpose is to work together.

As the IIA states in their mission statement, Internal Audit exists to "enhance and protect organizational value by providing risk-based and objective assurance, advice, and insight."[2] "Enhance," "protect," "advice," "insight." These don't sound like the words of an uncaring organization, do they? Maybe your feelings toward Internal Audit are starting to thaw just a bit. If so, let's keep going.

The second paragraph of the IIA's definition of Internal Audit speaks toward why, beyond objectivity and independence, it's important and helpful to have auditing as a separate role. Why? Because Internal Audit brings unique expertise and perspective.

Auditors are experts in risk and controls. The client and the team being audited are likely not. Thus, a key benefit of Internal Audit is being able to utilize and capitalize on the unique expertise of auditors in relation to risks and controls in order to improve your processes and practices.

For example, an investment leader earned her role because of her expertise in alternative investments, connections with key players in the market, and leadership skills. That's what the organization wants her to focus on. If that leader is going to implement a new system to facilitate smoother management of the organization's investments, she should recognize that system implementation is not an area in which she has expertise. As such, she would bring in someone to manage the new system implementation (someone with the necessary expertise either within her organization or external to the organization). Doing so frees her up to focus on what she is charged with: managing the organization's alternative investments portfolio.

This concept applies to risk and control insights and assurance as well. To enable the investment leader to focus on managing the alternative investments portfolio, Internal Audit brings expertise on risk and control insights and assurance to the table. Combining everyone's individual areas of expertise leads to the development of stronger, more valuable products. Why would anyone say no to this partnership?

How Internal Audit Adds Value

Both internal auditors and their clients want their organization to succeed. Internal auditors add value by bringing a fresh, impartial perspective, free from biases that may cloud the judgment of those closer to the work of achieving business objectives. Internal auditors' impartiality, paired with having shared goals with the team and the organization, uniquely positions them to add value.

The IIA defines the value provided by Internal Audit as assurance, insight, and objectivity. The IIA expands on this:

> Management and governing bodies can look to their internal auditors to provide assurance on whether policies are being followed, controls are effective, and the organization is operating as management intends.

Internal auditors have unique insight on which risks might lead to disaster; how to improve controls, processes, procedures, performance, and risk management; and ways to reduce costs, enhance revenues, and increase profits. And internal auditors view the organization with the strictest sense of objectivity that separates them from — but makes them integral to — the business.[3]

Organizations need both functional teams and Internal Audit to achieve their objectives. Teams need internal auditors focused on evaluating key risks and controls so team members can focus on delivering business results.

Internal auditors evaluate key risks and controls, either through assurance or consulting activities. Assurance activities are the most common type of audit activities. These are what you typically think of as an audit, where the auditors evaluate key risks[*] and the design and operating effectiveness of key controls[†] in a given process. The intended outcome of an assurance engagement is to assure the organization that key controls are designed and operating effectively, or that the process performs as expected, as well as to communicate any audit observations.[‡] In other words, auditors look at an organization's processes to see whether they're working the way the organization thinks they're working (or needs them to work in order to succeed).

During *consulting* activities, sometimes referred to as advisory services, internal auditors often advise their clients on how they might improve their processes, reduce risk, increase security, and better position themselves to achieve their objectives. Examples of consulting activities include pre-implementation reviews, training, providing advice on policies or processes, and other procedures to be performed that are agreed upon between the auditors and audit clients. Again, the value that Internal Audit provides here is their expertise in risks and controls, their knowledge of the broader organization (because of their experiences auditing processes and products across the organization), and their fresh perspective. After all, an experienced auditor has seen dozens of different ways of operating

---

* Risk is simply something that could cause harm to the organization or prevent it from succeeding. An example of a risk is the possibility that someone will walk into a bank and steal all the bank's cash on hand.

† "Key controls" simply means actions taken to prevent the risk from happening or detect it when it happens and fix it. Following along with the previous example, if the risk is that someone walks into a bank and steals all the bank's cash on hand, key controls would be storing the cash in a vault, securing the vault with a lock, and safeguarding the key or code that enables one to open the vault's lock.

‡ Audit observations are gaps between the current state (how something is actually being done) and the expected state of a process or control (how it's supposed to be done).

in a number of unique situations. They can bring this wealth of experience and expertise to help you find the best way to operate in your unique environment.

Their fresh perspective is also a great tool to leverage. Because they aren't involved in the nitty-gritty business operations every day, they can often ask questions that help the client think about things a little differently. These questions can spark the team to consider things they hadn't previously considered or identify ways to do things differently. We can all fall victim to the "that's how we've always done it" trap, continuing with certain practices simply because that's how we did it in the past.[*] An auditor's fresh perspective can question those practices, helping their clients see that while those practices may have made sense a while ago, perhaps they no longer do. Maybe there's a different way of doing things that can be more effective or efficient.

Often, this *advice* is seen as a dictate or that there is only one way of operating effectively, but that simply isn't true. That's why this type of work is called *consulting*. Auditors *consult* with their clients to *recommend* improvements. They aren't *mandating* anything.

An Organization's Three Lines

The IIA introduced the Three Lines Model as an update to its previous Three Lines of Defense model. In a 2020 position paper, the IIA introduced its Three Lines Model to help "organizations identify structures and processes that best assist the achievement of objectives and facilitate strong governance and risk management."[4] Essentially, it's guidance for organizations on how to structure various teams in the organization to strengthen the organization's ability to manage risks effectively.

The first line in this model is accountable for the organization's processes and products and managing the organization's risks. This would be the organization's management team. The second line in this model helps the first line manage risks, typically through setting organizational risk policies and evaluating the effectiveness with which risk is managed. Often, this is a risk management or internal controls function like quality assurance or quality control or a compliance organization. Internal Audit is the third line in this model, providing independent assurance to the organization's governing body.

---

[*] Auditors can fall victim to this trap too. That's one of the main points in this book: auditors have continued to perform audits the same way they always have, and while that used to work very well in the past, we need to think about audit work from a new perspective. This book provides that different perspective and offers advice on how to improve the audit process.

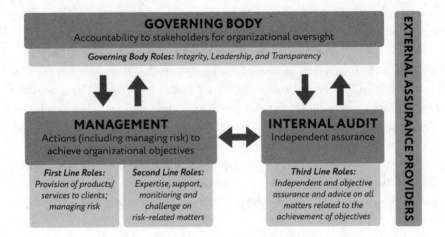

Figure 1.1: The IIA's Three Lines Model
Reproduced from Institute of Internal Auditors. *The IIA's Three Lines Model: An Update of the Three Lines of Defense*. The Institute of Internal Auditors: Lake Mary, FL: 2020. https://www.theiia.org/globalassets/documents/resources/the-iias-three-lines-model-an-update-of-the-three-lines-of-defense-july-2020/three-lines-model-updated-english.pdf.

As part of the same organization as the client, internal auditors differ from external auditors, who are part of a separate organization. It's also important to distinguish between internal auditors (often referred to as the third-line function) and other internal assurance providers (commonly referred to as second-line functions), such as risk management and compliance teams.

Like internal audit, second-line functions are part of the same organization as the first line and are often charged with providing assurance and insights to their clients over risks and controls. Some second lines are also accountable for setting policies, standards, and risk tolerances.

Internal Audit and second-line functions differ primarily in their reporting structures and scopes of coverage. Internal Audit has a more independent reporting structure than do second lines. This is typically accomplished through Internal Audit's reporting relationship with the organization's board of directors (or a committee of the board). This creates a layer of independence, which enables internal auditors to carry out their work without fear of repercussions from management (in the Three Lines Model, management refers to the first or second lines), which could impede the auditors' ability to provide objective assurance. Internal auditors do not define policies, standards, or risk tolerances for the organization.

Internal auditors have a broad scope that covers the entire organization, while second lines have a more narrowed focus. Both have their advantages. The narrow scope of second-line functions enables those teams to stay closer to the first line and dive deeper into the areas within their scope. While reporting structures differ with second lines, these teams ultimately report through the client or management. This could lead to reduced objectivity. Internal Audit's broad scope enables a more independent and objective lens. The combination of effective second- and third-line functions provides an organization with both depth and breadth of coverage, as well as appropriate levels of objectivity.

How Internal Auditing Works Today

Internal Audit exists to "enhance and protect organizational value by providing risk-based and objective assurance, advice, and insight."[5] In most organizations today, auditors carry out this mission by using a fairly standard and rigid process (a traditional waterfall audit approach) that adheres to standards set forth by the IIA. These standards include requirements about the attributes of internal auditors and Internal Audit organizations, as well as requirements outlining how internal auditing activities should be performed.

Before we move on to improving the audit experience, I think it's important to clearly explain how and why auditors work as they do today. If you're an experienced auditor, you may choose to skip over this section. For nonauditors, this section can be valuable to you to help you understand the process historically used to conduct audits.

Traditional Audit Approach

Traditionally, audits are performed in stages, with the audit team completing one stage before moving to the next stage. This is known as a waterfall approach (which should look very familiar to anyone in software development or project management). In audit work, the waterfall flows like this: planning, fieldwork, reporting, and, finaly, follow-up. Typical audits in large, complex organizations last around three months, inclusive of the planning, fieldwork, and reporting phases.

Figure 1.2:
Traditional Waterfall Audit Process

Using the waterfall approach, auditors begin with the **planning stage**, where they gain a high-level understanding of the process or technology under review. This occurs at the beginning of the audit, and auditors identify all of the key risks and controls relevant to the area under review. This is usually done with some guidance from the team being audited, but is mostly conducted by auditing in a silo. For each of the controls determined to be in the audit's scope, the audit team documents test procedures and gets audit leadership's approval to proceed. The idea here is to build a great plan and stick to it.

Once the audit is planned out and approved, the auditors move to the **field-work stage** of the audit. During this stage, the audit staff tests all of the in-scope controls and draws conclusions on the effectiveness of these controls. To keep things moving, auditors typically have a large portion of the control tests in process concurrently. As you might guess, a lot of multitasking happens at this stage. All control testing must be complete and approved by audit leadership before moving on to the reporting phase. The fieldwork stage of an internal audit can take anywhere from one week to several weeks, and in extreme cases can take up to several months.[6]

Once conclusions are reached on all in-scope controls, the audit team moves to the **reporting stage**. It typically takes between one and four weeks to complete this stage. Here, the audit team compiles the results, including audit observations, into an audit report. Again, compilation of the report is conducted by the auditors in a silo, with little to no interaction with the client. Once complete, the audit team distributes a draft of the report to the organization's key stakeholders. This is where things can get heated.

Because the audit was performed in silos, audit clients are sometimes surprised by the results delivered in the report. With that, negotiations begin, with auditors clinging to the gaps they identified and nonauditors rallying for the language or the ratings assigned to observations in the report to be modified. Auditors argue that the gaps are significant to the organization, and their clients argue that they're irrelevant or not as important as the auditors are making them out to be.

The rounds and rounds of revising the report and quarreling over seemingly minor items in the report further extend the length of time between identifying a gap and the audit clients actually addressing the gap. Suddenly, it becomes more about winning and proving your adversary wrong than helping the organization achieve its objectives. Finally, after weeks of negotiations that you thought would never end, the auditors deliver the final audit report.

From there is the **follow-up stage**. In this stage, auditors follow up on the observations delivered in that final audit report, determining whether their clients are taking action to address the identified gaps. Many auditors and clients think the core audit work is complete once the report is issued. If the team identified observations during the audit, there's still plenty of work left during the follow-up stage, both for auditors and clients. In fact, one of my colleagues put it well: "Once the audit report is issued, that's when the real work begins."

During this stage, it can be easy for auditors and clients to lose sight of the observations identified during the audit, as regular, day-to-day work resumes. For the client, that's their normal business operations. For the auditors, it's off to the next audit. Because of this, conflicts can arise during the follow-up stage as well.

Problems with the Traditional Internal Audit Approach

This waterfall approach has been a successful approach for decades, but it presents some challenges in today's world. In the past, this framework worked well because risks were fairly static. There were rarely changes to the organization's goals or products between the time the audit started and was completed. The risks remained the same year after year, so it was easy for the audit team to conduct the same audit over and over again. This is still true in some areas, and the traditional waterfall approach can still be successful in these unique cases.

But in most areas today, risks are changing at a velocity previously unseen. This new environment creates unique challenges for auditors, including:

- Difficulty in adjusting the approved scope to accommodate changes once fieldwork has begun
- Limited pockets of feedback during the audit
- Communication breakdowns
- Lengthy periods of time between identifying gaps and communicating gaps to the client

These limitations can result in stress (for both the auditors and the client), impediments to achieving objectives (which is the exact opposite of what clients and auditors both want), and an adversarial (or challenging, at best) relationship between auditors and their clients.

In the past, most audit work was repetitive and known. Auditors would primarily focus on financial statement audits or compliance audits, where the year-over-year scope would remain relatively similar. The prior year's list of risks and controls typically served as the list of risks and controls to cover in the current year's audit. An example of this type of audit is one focused on determining compliance with the Sarbanes-Oxley Act (i.e., SOX audits), where the controls and test procedures rarely changed from period to period.

These types of audits are still performed today; however, the risk landscape has drastically changed, transformed by a number of influences, including the COVID-19 pandemic and the digital revolution. Both the pandemic and the digital revolution have changed the way organizations conduct business and operate. Many risks that are present today weren't present or as prevalent a few decades ago, such as risks associated with the following:

- Large-scale remote or hybrid workforce models
- Global cybersecurity
- Connected devices and the Internet of Things
- Climate change
- Organizational reliance on artificial intelligence, machine learning, and automation
- Transition from on-premises technology infrastructure hosting models to cloud-based or hybrid hosting models

This is definitely not an exhaustive list, but you get the gist: we're all facing more risks, and they're being introduced at a much faster pace than we've historically experienced. Additionally, many audit clients are working with agility, and the old control mindset no longer works in these situations.

In response, the audit profession expanded its scope to include many more types of audits, including those assessing risks beyond compliance and financial reporting risks, such as operational risks, strategic risks, and environmental risks. Some of these audits cover areas where the work is more unique and less predictable than in SOX and compliance-focused audits. However, expanding the scope of audits is not enough; auditors need to modify their approach as well.

Auditors can no longer cling to an approach that does not enable them to accommodate change or understand how teams work today. PwC, a professional services firm, poses a thought-provoking question: "When nothing in the internal or external environment is status quo, isn't it time to think differently about internal audit?"[7] They advocate for thinking about auditing differently by highlighting an audit team that "identifies high risk transactions with channel partners, [in] real time, to fundamentally change the scope and approach of the audit."[8] PwC doubles down on this by closing with the following:

For the internal audit function, avoiding change is not an option. Transforming itself is not only what the business needs, it's crucial to the function's contribution to the enterprise, not to mention its continuing relevance to the business.[9]

PwC isn't alone in this perspective. A 2021 article by McKinsey furthers the argument by stating,

As the risk landscape becomes more complex, the onus is on IA functions to review their current operations—ensuring they are equipped for a working landscape that, in some areas, has seen years of change in just a few months.[10]

With an ever-changing environment, an audit approach that encourages flexibility and the ability to respond to change is superior to and provides more value than one that operates with rigidity.

To further illustrate this, consider the traditional waterfall audit approach. The timeline for completing these audits may span anywhere from a few months to a year, depending on the organization. Auditors following this approach invest time in the beginning of the audit to understand the control environment and identify key risks and control points for the entire process or technology under review.

There is a problem with applying this approach in today's ever-changing and unpredictable environment, as Jonathan Smart explains in *Sooner Safer Happier: Antipatterns and Patterns for Business Agility*:

Due to the long duration of traditional projects, the control environment is likely to have changed since initiation, with new controls to implement. For this to be discovered late in the life cycle leads to unplanned work, [and] delays. . .[11]

While Smart is not referring directly to audit projects, his statement accurately captures the essence of what auditors and clients can experience when using a waterfall approach.

An audit managed using the traditional approach sets the stage for the audit "at a time when the least information is known."[12] Auditors gain a high-level understanding of the controls within the process during the planning stage; however, deeper knowledge is gained during fieldwork, when the auditors dive deeper into the specifics of the process and supporting controls. When the auditors are best positioned to determine the detailed scope of an audit, they're already deep into the testing phase. Changes to the scope at this point typically lead to extending the audit beyond original deadlines and require approval for the changes (resulting in unplanned work for both the auditors and the client), if the auditors recognize the need to change.

According to an IIA Financial Services brief on Agile Auditing, Capital One (a publicly held, US-based bank with over 50,000 employees[13]) experienced challenges with the traditional audit approach, both from the auditor's perspective and across the rest of the organization.

The challenges faced by the *clients* included:[14]

- The need to periodically reeducate auditors
- Lack of consistency in the audit "rules of engagement"
- High volume of requests and questions toward the end of the audit
- Lack of visibility into the results of the audit until the audit team revealed the draft audit report

Capital One's *auditors* also experienced challenges with the traditional audit approach, including:[15]

- Limited time for research and education prior to engagement
- Information not available in a timely manner
- Elongated delivery cycle times
- Waterfall report reviews and revisions
- No break between audits—auditors ran from one to the next

This example shows that both auditors and audit clients are negatively impacted by clinging to the way audits have always been conducted and applying one rigid audit approach in every situation without accounting for the uniqueness of the processes or products under review. On a positive note, it shows a commonality between the two historically opposing sides, auditors and clients, but that's the only positive thing I'm seeing here.

There are far more negative impacts, like pulling audit clients away from their daily work to accommodate unplanned work in the form of numerous unexpected audit requests, delayed delivery of value (thus reducing the value of what's delivered), and burnout. The negative effects far outweigh the positive ones.

More Challenges with Traditional Waterfall

The challenges with applying the traditional waterfall audit approach to every situation in today's environment are abundant.

Organizations such as the *Journal of Accountancy* and Wolters Kluwer, as well as thought leaders on internal auditing, such as Norman Marks, cite the following challenges:

- ". . . if they don't completely understand the risks of the business, internal auditors can perform only traditional checklist tasks."[16]
- "Internal Audit has a long-standing reputation [of being] compliance police who come around every year with a standard checklist. Unfortunately, some auditors perpetuate this stereotype by auditing with checklists and canned audit programs without considering processes and risks."[17]
- "Too many audit reports produced by audit managers are written to be overly complicated and filled with jargon and acronyms. Often the meaning of the issue is lost from trying to sound smart."[18]
- "The controls and testing approach are excessive or are not targeted in the right areas. In other words, auditors are actually wasting time (and shareholder dollars)."[19]
- "Auditing risks that don't matter to the board and top executives."[20]
- "The traditional way of communicating audit results is a formal written report issued weeks if not months after issues are identified. The report says what internal audit wants to say rather than what management and the board need to know."[21]
- "An inability to change direction as risks change. . . . If you don't have the ability to modify the audit plan rapidly and frequently, what assurance is there that you are auditing what matters today and tomorrow?"[22]
- "Wasting precious time and resources."[23]
- "Failing to attain and retain the confidence of management. . . . If management does not believe we are helping them succeed, why should they support us?"[24]

I can't bear to list any more. It's heartbreaking enough to see those challenges listed out in one place, let alone to think about the audit clients who have experienced these challenges first-hand.

Let's explore one of my personal experiences with the traditional audit approach. Keep in mind that this is from my experience at a large, complex organization. It highlights an atypically long and complex audit. Not all audits are this long. What I want you to walk away with is what we all (auditors and audit clients) experienced when using the traditional audit approach. It's also important to note that although this example highlights the challenges my team and I faced using the waterfall approach in a highly complex audit, if you blindly apply a waterfall approach to a less complex audit, you may experience a similar outcome.

ADVENTURES IN AUDITING
Traditional Audit of IAM Technology Team

By the middle of 2019, I was about six months into my new role leading the technology audit team at a Fortune 100 company. I was new to the technology world. Each day, I spent my commutes listening to audio training courses and YouTube videos (audio only) on technology, trying to learn as much as I could.

Thankfully, I was very familiar with the audit process. As an auditor, it didn't matter what team I was on or which part of the organization I was auditing, the audit process always stayed the same. It would soon become clear to me that this was not a good thing.

It was around this time that the organization's identity and access management (IAM) process was due to be audited. If you're in technology, you know that IAM is critical for any organization. It ensures the right people have access to the information they need to do their jobs and help the organization achieve its objectives. It ensures the organization's customers can access their information to conduct business with the organization as well. It also prevents bad actors from accessing and exploiting an organization's data and resources, including customer data. Proper IAM practices support maintaining and preserving confidentiality, integrity, and availability of an organization's data and resources.

Because of its significance, the IAM audit usually gets a lot of visibility with key stakeholders. IAM is also a key component of many SOX compliance programs, so an organization's external auditors are typically quite interested in the IAM audit as well.

Despite the high-profile nature of the audit, my team and I were confident in our abilities. After all, an audit was an audit. The process was always the same.

First, we drafted our audit scope by consulting industry publications from the Institute of Internal Auditors and ISACA* on best practices for auditing IAM. Next, we met with key members of the IAM team to gain a high-level understanding of key risks and controls relevant to IAM at our organization. After a few weeks, my team felt they had comprehensively documented the key risks and controls they planned to cover and the steps they would take to test those controls.

The team gained the required approvals and presented the scope to our clients, the IAM team, informing them of what we would be covering during the audit. (Notice how we told the IAM team what we would be auditing. This will be important later.)

In true waterfall audit fashion, we then began fieldwork, where we tested the in-scope controls. Over the course of the next few months (yes, I said months), my team conducted walkthroughs with leaders of the team to understand how the in-scope controls were designed and to follow up on the status of the client's efforts to fulfill the audit team's requests for evidence, which had been provided at the time my team presented the scope to our clients.

However, here the trouble began. In some cases, the client provided my team data or evidence that wasn't what we actually needed. We thought our requests were clear, but they obviously were not. This communication breakdown led to delays. In some cases, it took my team several attempts before we received the data or evidence we needed to begin testing the operating effectiveness of the in-scope controls.

Once we had the information we needed, we were able to begin testing and reviewing the evidence. We presented our observations to the IAM management team in meetings every two weeks. After a few rounds of back-and-forth between my team and the client over the course of another two weeks, we finally agreed on the wording and rating for that particular audit observation.

Then we continued testing the other in-scope controls, presenting results to the client along the way during those status meetings, over and over again until we had tested everything in scope. This took upward of three months.

Finally, my team was ready to compile the audit report and present it to the client in a closing/exit meeting. We were proud of the work we had completed over the last several months, and we were confident that we

---

* ISACA (formerly the Information Systems Audit and Control Association) is a professional organization that helps technology professionals realize technology's potential.

were delivering a report that would help the IAM team conduct their work with less risk. We were helping.

During the closing/exit meeting, as we walked through the draft audit report, the client immediately began questioning our audit observations, even those we had previously presented and negotiated with them.

Then, different teams within IAM negotiated with each other to determine the owners of the audit observation. Pinpointing an accountable party for each audit observation was quite difficult. Executives from the IAM team present didn't fully buy into the audit observations and disagreed with the ratings assigned to the audit observations. It was a tense meeting and a classic case of auditors versus client.

Eventually, we reached a point where we could issue the final audit report. Phew. We were done. It's safe to say that both sides were happy to move on from this particular audit.

As was standard practice, my team sent surveys to the IAM team to obtain feedback on their audit experience. We auditors see ourselves as helpers. We want to make the experience better. Unfortunately, the feedback indicated that the client didn't find much value in the audit or the results communicated in the report.

This was disheartening. It was like being told that all your hard work was worthless.

I am completely confident in the work my team did. They complied fully with the IIA's Standards and with our audit organization's policies and procedures. The audit scope was comprehensive, and the team's conclusions were accurate and well supported. My team successfully provided assurance on key controls within the IAM program and clearly communicated control gaps identified during the audit. It was everything a good audit should be.

Yet we faced a number of challenges along the way, and in the end the value we delivered wasn't clear. So where had we gone wrong?

Reflecting on the experience outlined above, it is a fairly one-sided view of the audit, not considering the client's perspective. That pretty much sums up the audit itself—a number of missed opportunities to collaborate more closely and work as one team, as opposed to working in silos. Well, we requested evidence of control performance and data for control testing before understanding how the control was designed. No wonder our clients provided the wrong evidence. We set them up for failure! We also developed the audit scope primarily in a silo, with only minimal input from the client. No wonder we didn't have a ton of buy-in on the control gaps we identified! They didn't get a chance to buy into the scope to begin with! There was also a lot of switching from one task to another and then switching back to the original task, particularly with audit observations. We didn't collaborate as closely with our clients on information requests as we should have. No wonder there were delays in getting the right information! We missed countless opportunities to more clearly understand and articulate what we were looking for.

It was clear that the hard work my team had conducted didn't register as value to the IAM team. In fact, it seemed the whole experience had only caused more strife, arguments, bottlenecks, and adversaries. I started thinking about what we could do differently to avoid or address some of these challenges in future audits. There had to be another way.

Chapter 2

Journey toward Agile Auditing

As we saw in Chapter 1, the traditional waterfall method of internal auditing worked for decades. But in today's rapidly changing environment, the approach no longer serves the organization well in many instances. It is long and inflexible and oftentimes drives adversarial relationships between two teams that *should* be working together.

The IIA's 2018 North American Pulse of Internal Audit survey results emphasized the importance of adding agility to auditing.[1] Internal Audit groups in every industry were looking to this idea of agility in auditing as a way to combat the novel challenges that had cropped up with the digital revolution, including the changing business landscape, increased velocity of risks, new and emerging risks, new technology, and increased uncertainty.

At the time of the survey, respondents indicated that although the importance of agility was clear, there were roadblocks to achieving the desired levels of agility in auditing, including resource challenges, organizational complexity, limited availability of the client for collaboration, and traditional expectations key stakeholders have of auditors.[2]

It was also unclear *how* to achieve agility and what success really looked like. This isn't uncommon with emerging concepts: the *why* is often clear, the *what* is somewhat clear, while the *how* is often unknown. This was no different. Auditors knew why they needed to change: the environment had changed, and traditional ways of working weren't keeping up. They understood that agility and the ability to adapt to changes and keep up in the new environment was the answer (the what). What they hadn't quite figured out was how. Enter the sprint-based delivery model known today as Agile Auditing.

What Is Agile Auditing?

To anyone in the manufacturing or software development industries, Agile should be fairly well known. Agile is defined by the Agile Alliance as "the ability to create and respond to change. It is a way of dealing with, and ultimately succeeding in, an uncertain and turbulent environment."[3] Agile gained popularity as an approach to software development, anchored in values and principles to help teams navigate uncertainty and change. (I've provided more information on the Agile Values and Principles in the Appendix.) Because of the success the audit profession witnessed in other parts of their organizations where teams practiced Agile, auditors looked to apply Agile concepts to the audit process.

Agile Auditing became a project management framework that intended to provide a consistent or continual approach to auditing, performed iteratively in sprints instead of delivering only at the end of the audit. Organizations began experimenting with this approach in 2016, and it gained significant airtime in the industry beginning around 2017, with a number of papers published introducing the topic, including:

- *Agile Auditing: Sprinting to Change: Reimagining Internal Audit in a Digital World*, published by the IIA in 2018[4]
- *Becoming Agile: A Guide to Elevating Internal Audit's Performance and Value*, released by Deloitte in 2017[5]
- *Agile Auditing: Mindset over Matter*, released by PwC in 2018[6]

Articles in the IIA's *Internal Auditor Magazine* included articles on Agile Auditing from 2019 through today. These articles focused on delivering audits in sprints and leveraging Scrum concepts, such as sprint planning, daily stand-ups, and sprint reviews, during an audit. Industry webinars also focused primarily on performing audits in sprints as the go-to framework for Agile Auditing.

Today, most Agile Audits are performed by breaking the audit timeline into a number of sprints, typically lasting two weeks each. Each sprint includes elements of planning, fieldwork, and reporting, with results delivered at the end of each sprint. Agile Audits leverage daily stand-ups, where the team provides an update on the status of their work and communicates roadblocks or impediments to progress. Agile Audit teams perform a retrospective review at the end of each sprint to identify ways to improve in the next sprint.

CASE STUDY Anywhere Real Estate Inc.[7]

Anywhere Real Estate Inc.'s Internal Audit team performs all of their audits using the Agile Auditing framework. The organization's

Internal Audit team leverages the following roles on each audit: Scrum Master, Product Owner, and Scrum Team Member. The Scrum Master roles are either performed by the audit manager or a more experienced audit staff member and hold a Scrum Master certification. Their primary roles are to coach the audit team on Agile Auditing practices and ensure the audit is following the Agile Auditing framework.

By designating Scrum Masters for each audit and encouraging audit managers and experienced staff members to fulfill the role of Scrum Master, the team experienced "[g]reater staff engagement and buy-in" and "stretch opportunity for audit staff."[8]

Case studies across the auditing profession began popping up, showcasing organizations of various sizes using Agile Auditing, including larger organizations like Fidelity Investments (155 auditors), Siemens AG (260 auditors), and Walmart (325 auditors),[9] as well as smaller organizations, including Anywhere Real Estate (15 auditors).[10] With all this evidence and talk in the industry, I knew I had to give Agile Auditing a try.

ADVENTURES IN AUDITING
Agile Auditing, Take One

Let's go back to my story at the Fortune 100 company. After my first less-than-optimal audit with the IAM team in 2019, I knew we had to look for new ways of working. Agile Auditing as a concept was sweeping the audit profession. While the benefits of this concept were well articulated, there was a lack of clarity on what exactly it was and how to implement it. So my team and I embarked on a series of experiments into Agile Auditing ways of working to discover if and how it could work for us.

In the second half of 2020 and into the first quarter of 2021, my team participated in an audit project testing specific controls in partnership with the organization's external auditors. This was a high-profile project with a lot of attention from our organization's key stakeholders and a tight time frame within which testing had to be completed. The tight timeline drove the need for my team to think about our work differently. Because the team was testing on behalf of another party, continuous feedback and the ability to pivot quickly was imperative. It quickly became clear that this project was a strong candidate in which to implement Agile practices.

We set out on our first experiment into Agile Auditing by focusing on three key elements:

- Avoid multitasking
- Incorporate continuous delivery in short sprints
- Work with the client through iterative meetings and daily stand-ups

To avoid multitasking, our team was composed of dedicated individuals who focused primarily on this engagement. The team's priority was crystal clear, so we spent less time reevaluating priorities than is typical when juggling multiple projects. This differed from our normal operating model, where each audit staff member typically worked on anywhere from two to six audits at once.

We also used continuous delivery to work in short sprints. We divided testing into four blocks of time that we called "buckets." We specified a number of controls to test in each bucket, and each bucket lasted approximately one month (there was some variation from bucket to bucket). This time-boxed approach encouraged a sense of urgency with both the audit team and the client.

In an effort to work more closely with the client and to work iteratively, we updated internal stakeholders (the control owners/clients) weekly on the status of the work and any audit observations we wanted to share with them. The audit team then met with external stakeholders (the external auditors) twice each week, sent out detailed meeting notes to reiterate key decisions reached, and sought feedback and confirmation from those stakeholders after each meeting. This kept us all aligned on progress made and next steps. In addition, the audit team held daily stand-up meetings that supported flexibility and reinforced the urgency and priority of the audit. These stand-ups enabled the team to

- seek and address feedback continually,
- shift available resources to tasks that needed attention,
- share knowledge among the team, and
- change testing procedures on the fly to adapt to stakeholder needs.

At the end of the third bucket, we conducted a retrospective review to reflect on how to become more effective in the final bucket. The team identified a number of ways to improve the process, including

- conducting weekly stand-ups with key management points of contact to enable even more timely and streamlined discussions, and
- consolidating the team's questions for the external audit team and discussing them during the weekly meetings when all relevant decision-makers were present (to increase consistency in feedback and direction given).

Even though we had some great success with this audit, it still wasn't perfect. Because we didn't have consistent involvement from key parties in weekly meetings, we miscommunicated at times, resulting in duplicate efforts and unnecessary rework. We also hadn't expanded our feedback loops to include representation from all teams involved, such as the external auditors. This led to certain inefficiencies that didn't improve throughout the audit.

But as the project drew to a close at the end of the final bucket, I no longer asked myself whether Agile concepts *could* translate to the world of auditing. Now the question was, how far could we go to achieve even greater value?

Benefits of Agile Auditing

As my first experiment with Agile Auditing came to a close, I refocused on what the primary goal of Agile Auditing was. In my opinion, it mainly promised increased efficiency by reducing the amount of time spent during an audit, namely in the reporting stage of an audit (the time between the end of testing and when the final audit report is published). Because results during an Agile Audit are delivered iteratively throughout the audit rather than all at the end, the client is familiar with Internal Audit's observations before the final report is drafted. This often results in fewer negotiations on the contents of the report and a faster or more efficient reporting stage.

In turn, this gets audit results into the clients' hands sooner so they can start addressing the audit observations earlier. By the time the final report is published, the client has likely already begun making progress in addressing the observations, so auditors can include that progress in the final audit report, which in turn tells a much better story to the organization's key stakeholders.

Thus, I find that another benefit of Agile Auditing is that it can create the opportunity for organizations to address risk exposures *sooner*. In my own personal experience, my clients made significantly more progress addressing gaps identified during the audit (i.e., my audit clients had accepted the risk or had a plan in place to address the risk, or better yet, they had already addressed the risk and closed the gap) as compared to an audit in the same space two years prior using the traditional waterfall approach.

CASE STUDY Anywhere Real Estate Inc.

Becca Kinney (SVP Internal Audit at Anywhere Real Estate Inc.) and Dan Greenfield (Agile Internal Audit Manager at Anywhere Real Estate Inc.) experienced incredible efficiencies when moving from a waterfall audit approach to Agile Auditing. Using the traditional waterfall approach to auditing, the reporting phase of the audit would often take 100 days or more. After implementing Agile Auditing, the time spent in Anywhere Real Estate Inc.'s audit reporting phase was cut significantly to an average of twenty days. That's an 80% decrease in the amount of time spent negotiating on the audit report![11]

In addition, the team's final audit reports often show progress the client has made on observations identified and communicated earlier in the audit (delivered in interim audit reports). The client has responded positively to this improvement, as their auditors recognize and publish their efforts and progress toward mitigating risks in the audit report.

As I dove into researching Agile Auditing further, I found that an additional benefit was that organizations leveraging Agile Auditing experienced less burden on clients due to increased knowledge sharing. In an ISACA publication titled *Destination: Agile Auditing*, Dawn Vogel of Nelnet, Inc., indicated that through Agile Auditing, her team "leveraged knowledge shared during standups [sic] to avoid asking clarifying questions of auditees, which allowed more time for delivering value to customers."[12]

Finally, Michael Podemski of professional services firm Aon's audit organization cited the following in ISACA's *Destination: Agile Auditing*: "Involving the customer allows our team to focus on developing an audit backlog containing relevant focus areas which are risky to the business and helps us avoid increasing audit risk leading to engagement failure."*[13]

I was starting to see that there was something more to this Agile Auditing idea. But as with any new methodology or idea, there were as many challenges as there were benefits.

Challenges with Agile Auditing

In 2018, the IIA surveyed 636 chief audit executives (CAEs). Only 45% of respondents (including representatives from financial services industries and nonfinancial services industries) indicated that they were "very" or "extremely" Agile.[14] The IIA explains that this indicates a gap between what CAEs see as important and how much they've invested in addressing it.

In addition, AuditBoard indicated in 2020 that as a profession, auditors hadn't made much progress in figuring out how to reap the benefits of agility:

> A recent AuditBoard poll of over 1,000 internal auditors found that 82% say agile auditing has the potential to add more value to their work compared to the traditional project approach—although 45% reported a lack of knowledge or resources as the most significant obstacle to adopting agile.[15]

Furthermore, Deloitte conducted a survey on the use of Agile Auditing and published the results of this survey in October 2021. According to the survey, 45% of the 181 organizations who responded to the survey were leveraging or considering Agile Auditing.[16] Deloitte concluded, based on the survey results, that Agile Auditing is "helping functions to achieve better impact, faster insight, and happier and more engaged stakeholders."[17] Figure 2.1 (on page 28) shows the percentage of survey respondents who had experienced various benefits associated with Agile Auditing.

Based on the surveys (2018 IIA Pulse of Internal Audit Survey, 2020 AuditBoard survey, and 2021 Deloitte survey), Agile Auditing had taken hold in less than half of survey respondents between 2018 and 2021. Those leveraging Agile Auditing reported experiencing clear benefits, such as greater impact, faster

---

* An audit backlog is a list of what needs to be done to complete the audit.

delivery of insights, and greater stakeholder engagement. Why, then, had more organizations not embraced Agile Auditing?

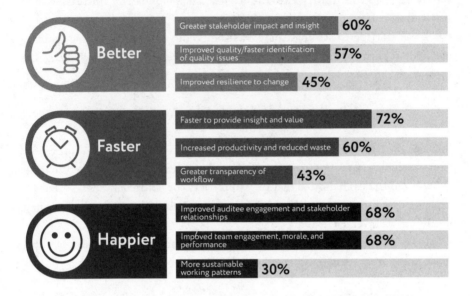

Figure 2.1: The Percentage of Functions Reporting Benefits through Agile IA (by Benefit Category)
Reproduced from Deloitte. *Agile Internal Audit Four Years On: Better, Faster, Happier? A Retrospective.* Deloitte Development LLC, 2021. https://www2.deloitte.com/content/dam /Deloitte/global/Documents/Risk/gx-agile-internal-audit-four-years.pdf.

The Deloitte paper postulates that sprint-based Agile Auditing may not be the best approach for *all* audits.[18] It further explains various challenges survey respondents expressed in implementing Agile Auditing, including:

- Forcing teams to implement Agile Auditing and resistance to change
- Lack of clarity around the goal of Agile Auditing
- Inconsistent application of Agile Auditing among teams

This survey clearly showed that while Agile Auditing had been successfully adopted by a number of organizations, many were lagging behind, likely due to taking an all-or-nothing approach to Agile Auditing paired with a lack of buy-in with the audit teams.

Thinking Beyond Agile Auditing

While strict, sprint-based Agile Auditing works incredibly well for some audits and some organizations, its challenges show that Agile Auditing isn't a one-size-fits-all approach. Some teams may choose to implement this framework, while others may not. Still others may borrow some concepts from Agile Auditing and choose not to borrow other portions of it. Not one of these is the "best" way for everyone or for every audit. So if Agile Auditing wasn't the silver bullet, what is?

DevOps and Audit

Thinking back to my first week leading technology audit teams, I recall when one of my new clients approached me and asked if I would be interested in partnering with him on a presentation to our organization's technology department about DevOps.

I quickly responded, "Yes, of course! . . . Umm, what is DevOps?"

After some chuckling, my client suggested I read *The Phoenix Project: A Novel About IT, DevOps, and Helping Your Business Win*. I devoured the book in a few days, enthralled by the way it showed two adversarial teams (software developers and operations) struggling to work together. These two departments relied on each other to deliver value for their organization, but they struggled to communicate, actively hindered each other's work, and ultimately failed to deliver value. In fact, they often worked as outright enemies. To solve the problem, they instituted a mindset change: DevOps.

DevOps is an operating model where IT development and IT operations work together as one team with a collective goal of delivering value to customers. Before DevOps, development teams historically developed features and passed them over to the operations teams to run. The inherent problem with this is the disconnect between the two teams and often competing incentives for each, resulting in strained relationships between the two groups.

DevOps was first officially introduced in 2010 (following the 2009 presentation from John Allspaw and Paul Hammond).[19] This way of working enabled organizations to reduce the risk of software deployments, innovate, and offer more value to customers. Based on Lean and other principles that originated in the physical manufacturing industry, DevOps also builds upon the principles of Agile software development. DevOps brings together two parts of the organization that at times seem to be adversaries: development and operations.

In order to come together and work as one team, the two departments that are responsible for software development (Dev and Ops) seek to implement the Three Ways. The Three Ways is "a set of business principles that encourage organizations to value a corporate culture in which feedback loops are short, everyone understands how different parts of the business interrelate, and all employees are encouraged to seek knowledge that will help the company meet business goals."[20]

The First Way: Flow/Systems Thinking: According to *The Phoenix Project* coauthor Gene Kim, "The First Way emphasizes the performance of the entire system, as opposed to the performance of a specific silo of work or department."[21] *The DevOps Handbook* further explains that flow/systems thinking "accelerate[s] the delivery of work . . . to customers."[22]

The Second Way: Feedback Loops: Essentially, the Second Way is all about soliciting feedback from clients, making adjustments to address the feedback, and reducing the time it takes to obtain and address such feedback. In an IT Revolution blog post, Gene Kim defined the Second Way as:

> . . . creating the right to left feedback loops. The goal of almost any process improvement initiative is to shorten and amplify feedback loops so necessary corrections can be continually made. The outcomes of the Second Way include understanding and responding to all customers, internal and external, shortening and amplifying all feedback loops, and embedding knowledge where we need it.[23]

The Third Way: Continual Learning and Experimentation: *The DevOps Handbook* defines practices that enable the Third Way of DevOps, including:[24]

- Establishing a culture of organizational learning and safety
- Transforming local discoveries into global improvements
- Reserving time to create improvements and learning

After reading the book and attending conferences, I thought it appeared natural to apply the Three Ways of DevOps to auditing. Thus began my second experiment in Agile Auditing, this time incorporating elements of the Three Ways as well.

ADVENTURES IN AUDITING
Agile Auditing, Take Two: Incorporating the Three Ways

In my second experiment with Agile Auditing, we collaborated with a client who worked using Scrum and DevOps practices. So we kept going with a sprint-based audit delivery model, but this time with consistent sprint timeboxes. We also incorporated some DevOps concepts, like working together as one team (flow/systems thinking) and feedback loops.

This audit was staffed with only two of the same individuals (not including myself) who were on the first Agile Auditing experiment, so these concepts were completely new for most of the audit team. Through reading books geared toward technology organizations, as well as through coaching from the client, who was already well versed in using these practices, we set out to see if we could replicate some of the success from the first experiment and maybe do even better.

Another major change with our second experiment was to switch our mindset from auditors versus auditees. Instead of referring to ourselves as the "audit team" and the "client team," we collectively (everyone involved, including representatives from the client as well as Internal Audit) referred to ourselves as "THE team."

We were now one team with a collective goal: to determine whether key controls were designed and operating effectively within the area under review.

While this was a radical concept for the auditors involved, it wasn't too much of a stretch for the client. They had moved to a product-centric operating model a few years prior, so they had already integrated operations and risk management associates into the product team. This was simply the next step in their journey, even though it was more of a giant leap for the auditors.

We implemented the First Way of DevOps (Flow/Systems Thinking) by integrating the audit work into the client's daily work. Our rebranding to THE team reinforced the idea that we were committed to delivering value through providing assurance on a particular process's key controls, and everyone on THE team played an important role.

We also collaborated closely with the client on what areas we would focus on for the audit. This let the client plan for this work and adjust their commitments accordingly. Instead of the audit producing a lot of *unplanned* work for them, the First Way of DevOps facilitated *planned* work for the collective team.

We incorporated the Second Way (feedback loops) by intentionally soliciting feedback from THE team. We held retrospective reviews at the end of each sprint to identify what went well and what we wanted to improve in the next sprint. At the end of the entire audit, the auditors sent surveys to the client to collect additional feedback to be incorporated in our next audit. The high levels of collaboration on this audit also supported the exchange of real-time feedback. We immediately exchanged feedback within THE team, letting us pivot quickly to become more effective.

We learned the Third Way (continual learning and experimentation) the hard way. As we neared the end of the audit, we faced a significant challenge that caused us to revert to old ways of working.

When compiling the final audit report and determining the overall audit opinion, we reverted back to the auditor versus auditee operating model. We didn't experience that part of the audit together, as we had up until that point, because using the old ways of working put the client on the opposite side of the table from us. We were adversaries for a brief moment. To be completely vulnerable for a moment, this devastated me. We had worked so closely together during the audit and had so much fun along the way. To so quickly revert back to an adversarial relationship was heartbreaking.

Thankfully, we had built strong relationships throughout the audit, and we were all committed to the same goal of delivering value. We gave each other grace as we navigated this difficult situation, creating a culture that fostered taking risks and learning from failures. In this instance, our failure was leaving the client out of the process of compiling the final report and determining the overall audit opinion. Although the auditors had ultimate decision authority on that overall opinion, as with all other key decisions related to the audit work, we would have been even more effective if we had collaborated as one team during this final stage of the audit. We learned from this failure and came out on the other side of it stronger than before . . . TOGETHER.

In addition to the Three Ways of DevOps, we incorporated other better ways of working, such as increased visibility of work and daily stand-ups. The audit was an incredible success! When comparing key data points from the prior audit in this space, which followed the traditional waterfall audit process, the differences were astonishing. We provided more assurance (achieved 77% more coverage), and results were communicated and addressed sooner, all while spending 10% less calendar time on the audit. The surveys we sent to the client at the end of the audit also indicated incredibly positive feedback and high levels of client satisfaction. Suffice to say that this was an incredible success!

Looking Forward

Reflecting back on my Agile Auditing experiments, while there were way more positive results from implementing these better ways of working, it would be misleading to say the successes didn't come with challenges along the way.

Even with the reduction in multitasking we achieved in the attempt to audit in a DevOps way, the auditors on the team still had way too many tasks in process at the same time, as they were working on a large number of audits concurrently. Because of this, the team had to reorient themselves to the audit or the task at hand multiple times each day, as each day was filled with meetings pertaining to different audits and different tasks within each audit.

The team was also looking for a framework to follow. Luckily, the Agile Auditing framework, which is closely aligned with the Scrum framework, provided a sprint-based structure to follow.

Also, the auditors on the team were wary of working in new ways, for fear of violating professional internal auditing standards set forth by the IIA. We overcame this fear by expanding our team's membership to include someone well versed in the IIA's Standards. This individual gave us feedback along the way and answered our questions related to professional auditing standards. They helped us comply with the standards while adopting newer ways of working. The team progressed from saying, "We can't do this without violating the standards," to instead asking, "What can we do to work in this new way while meeting the requirements of the standards?"

We also intentionally prioritized the client's needs and fostered a collaborative environment. In our second experiment, we did this through intentionally collaborating with members of THE team throughout the audit. For example, we identified the audit's scope TOGETHER. Instead of the auditors using our traditional approach of having a few conversations with the client to get a high-level understanding of the area under review, going away to develop the audit scope, and then returning to present the scope to the client, we worked together to define scope boundaries and articulate the key risks and controls relevant to the area under review.

Taking it a step further, THE team determined the most effective way to test each of those controls and the evidence needed to test them. Those most familiar with the area under review (the clients) understood how the controls were performed and documented better than anyone else in the organization. So they were best positioned to help us determine how to test those controls, precisely what evidence was available, and where (or from whom) to obtain it.

We also incorporated the Agile concept of delivering results frequently. THE team delivered results at the conclusion of each sprint in an interim report, instead of waiting until the end of the audit. This enabled the client to begin addressing any audit observations earlier in the process rather than waiting until the end of a multiple-months-long audit. This resulted in the client addressing risk exposures sooner.

Working in this manner resulted in a better story to the organization's key stakeholders (recipients of the audit report). In the prior audit, when we delivered the final audit report, nearly all of the audit observations in the report were newly opened, and the client had made little to no progress addressing them. This is because the results weren't delivered to them throughout the audit; rather, they were all communicated at the end of the process. The story to key stakeholders was essentially, "Here are all of the control gaps that the client needs to address."

Conversely, the report delivered at the end of *this* audit told a completely different story. Most of the audit observations in the report were either remediated or were in the process of being remediated. The story to key stakeholders this time was, "Here are the control gaps we identified together. Look at how much progress the client has made already in addressing these! Great work, team!"

Chapter 3

Going beyond Agile Auditing

As we saw in the last chapter, Agile Auditing has both tangible and measurable benefits, but it also presents some challenges. One of the pitfalls of Agile Auditing is taking an all-or-nothing approach. In other words, many organizations turn what should be a mindset or cultural shift into yet another strict and rigid framework (so-called "Checklist Agile"). Other Agile Auditing mistakes include applying a rigid approach in every situation without accounting for the unique attributes of each area under review (i.e., assuming one size fits all); forcing teams to adopt a methodology, resulting in a resistance to change; focusing on the framework itself rather than the intended outcomes; and failing to consider the client's working style.

To truly reap the benefits that Agile Auditing promises us, we must move beyond the idea that Agile Auditing is a framework we can push onto our teams. We must move beyond the strict confines of Agile Auditing and toward that of, what I call, "Auditing with Agility." This subtle distinction is intentional and deserves some airtime.

Agile Auditing is often interpreted as a thing to do. Teams want to *do* Agile or do Agile audits. But with better ways of auditing, including Agile Auditing, *what* you do shouldn't change. Internal Audit should still provide assurance on existing risks and consult on emerging risks. Instead of something you do or a framework or method to employ, Auditing with Agility outlines ways to do what you do better. Using the phrase "Auditing with Agility" makes it more clear that what you do stays the same—you're still auditing. *How* you go about auditing is what changes, and it might not always be exactly the same in every instance.

You're not "doing" Agile, you're *being* agile.

"Doing" Agile is an output-focused approach, like measuring success by the number of audits performed in sprints or the number of audits that leverage daily stand-ups. Those measures don't directly correlate with value to the organization. Instead, *being* agile is a way of working focused on achieving outcomes, like increased ability to respond to change, delivery of results sooner, better alignment between audit activities and the most relevant or emerging risks, and increased ability to stop auditing when appropriate rather than continuing on the set path regardless of what the team learns along the way.

You can implement Agile tools and practices without being agile. It's important to change your mindset (and your organization's mindset) to one of agility (changing the way of working and thinking to enable adaptation to change) rather than a mindset focused on a single methodology.

The real benefits of Auditing with Agility are realized when you operate in an agile, adaptable manner, not necessarily when you implement a specific tool without modifying your processes to become more agile. What the digital revolution taught us is that an organization's ability to adapt to change is the number one differentiator on the market. It is the difference between failure and survival, as well as between surviving and thriving. If you're rigid and set in your ways, then change is a disruptor, sometimes with catastrophic results. However, if you're part of an adaptable organization, then change simply presents a new and welcome opportunity. This is what you live for. It doesn't have to be any different for Internal Audit.

Instead of every audit following the exact same waterfall approach, or every audit following the exact same Agile Auditing sprint formula, Auditing with Agility throws assumptions and strict frameworks out the window.

Instead, Auditing with Agility focuses on three core components: value, integration, and adaptability. I'm going to get into this more in the next chapter, but by focusing how we work on those three things, Internal Audit can face any change that's on the horizon.

Remember, this is only a change in how Internal Audit works, not in what Internal Audit does. Auditing with Agility still delivers independent, objective assurance and consulting services to add value and improve an organization's operations. Now we'll do it sooner, safer, and much happier.

Some organizations make a rapid switch from traditional ways of auditing straight to Agile Auditing, and as I stated earlier, some of these organizations fail in their transformations. Others, particularly those seeking to audit with agility rather than "doing" Agile Auditing, approach the transition as more of a journey. I was fortunate enough to be in one of those organizations.

In my third experiment with Agile Auditing, my team looked at the challenges from our previous two experiments and took things a bit further, including bringing in DevOps ways of thinking.

ADVENTURES IN AUDITING
Agile Auditing, Take Three

Following the success of our previous experiments in Agile Auditing, my team and I gained momentum with getting buy-in from Internal Audit leadership.

We began a third audit delivered in sprints, but the team built upon what we had learned in our previous Agile Auditing experiments, leveraging some of the behaviors and practices that worked successfully, as well as incorporating additional better ways of working.

This audit had some team members from the first sprint-based audit as well as some new, energized team members who were ready to experiment. We also had a different client: one that didn't leverage Agile, Scrum, or DevOps practices.

The auditors met with the client to provide a high-level overview of the modified audit process we were looking to implement. The overview focused on key mechanics (using team chats instead of endless meetings, high levels of collaboration instead of testing in silos, etc.) and benefits realized in the prior audits performed in this manner (rapid feedback, timely delivery of results, focus on the areas of greatest value, etc.).

Both the client and the auditors expressed concern to me about whether the area under review and the type of work the client performed lent itself to an agile approach to auditing. Admitting that I didn't have all the answers, I asked my team and our clients to proceed with an open mind and afford grace to each other as we navigated through the experiment. With a bit of hope mixed in with skepticism, we all embarked on the experiment together.

Throughout the audit, we continued to hold stand-ups; however, these were modified, as the collective team (auditors and the client) felt that daily meetings were too frequent. Instead, the auditors met three times each week without the client and once a week with the client.

We still successfully delivered the audit in three one-month-long sprints, and we continued to leverage a digital task board to make work visible. The collective team held retrospective reviews at the end of each sprint to reflect on and celebrate successes and learn from failures. We embraced psychological safety and the Third Way of DevOps, which maintained the excitement among our team. The feedback from the client via the end-of-audit survey also indicated a positive experience during the audit. Overall, the audit was a success.

From Agile Auditing to Auditing with Agility

After performing the third Agile Audit leveraging these better ways of working, I knew we were on to something bigger than just a new framework or methodology. We were going beyond Agile Auditing and discovering something new.

We continued experimenting with these tactics to varying degrees on subsequent audits. Some were delivered in sprints (using consistent timeboxes for delivery) and some were delivered in iterations where the time between delivery varied—triggered by something other than the expiration of a timebox. Yet others held delivery of finalized results until the end of the audit, with discussion of results with frontline client leaders throughout. During some audits, we integrated ourselves with the client and our work into the client's work more so than during others. Essentially, we chose the techniques and methods that would work best in each unique situation based on our desired outcomes.

For example, to enable more fluidity of staff between audits, we modified our task board to make our work more visible at a holistic, portfolio level rather than at the individual audit engagement level. To increase efficiency, the auditors joined the client's biweekly team meetings to request additional information and discuss results with client in real time, without adding more meetings to the client's calendar. To reduce disruptions caused by unplanned work, we worked with our clients to add audit-related tasks to their task board so they could consider those tasks during their backlog refinement sessions and plan for the audit work *with* their normal work.

As my team and I continued adopting better ways of working, we shared our stories with others in our organization and with auditors in other organizations. I also attended webinars and conference sessions devoted to Agile Auditing. From these discussions, webinars, and sessions, I picked up on a pattern: the auditing industry assumed that Agile was synonymous with Scrum and that Agile Auditing meant only performing audits in sprints. Further, the industry confused sprints with manageable chunks of work when in reality, sprints are timeboxes that may or may not have a one-to-one match with manageable chunks of work.

My team and I wondered whether the audit profession's assumption that Agile = Scrum was correct, so we experimented with adding agility to our work and integrating audit work into the client's work without delivering in sprints or following a strict Scrum or Agile Auditing framework. From this experimentation, we learned that while Agile Auditing is one way to add agility to audit work, it is not the only way.

To help create clarity on this, I started referring to our way of working as "Auditing with Agility" rather than Agile Auditing. I wanted our team to shift from thinking this is something you do (Agile Auditing seems to trigger thoughts of something you do) to thinking about it as a way of working (auditing in a manner that incorporates agility and leads to better outcomes).

We shifted from *Agile = Scrum* to *Auditing with Agility = auditing in a way that improves the ability to respond to change and makes the audit process flexible.*

Thanks to one of my mentors, I also realized that what we were doing went beyond agility by also incorporating the concept of performing value-driven work and integrating that work into the client's daily work.

In 2022, I presented at the DevOps Enterprise Summit, an annual conference for technology leaders. This time I didn't copresent with one of my audit teammates, as I had in previous years. Instead, I copresented with one of my clients. That's right, an auditor and a technology leader presented *together*—and had fun doing so.

After seeing my presentation for the first time, Gene Kim, coauthor of *The Phoenix Project* and founder of DevOps Enterprise Summit, reached out to me and my copresenter to express how startling he thought our presentation was. He shared that he thought we were on the "frontier of revolutionizing internal audit practices for the entire profession."[1] He likened it to the presentation given by John Allspaw and Paul Hammond at the 2009 Velocity conference. That 2009 presentation, titled "10 Deploys per Day: Dev and Ops Cooperation at Flickr,"[2] first introduced an operating model where technology developers and operations teams were no longer adversaries, but instead shared common goals and made technology development and operations part of both teams' work.

After watching that historic 2009 presentation, the parallels between that operating model and the one described in my 2022 presentation became clear. Even though I hadn't seen the 2009 presentation until after submitting my own. Gene was right . . . we were on to something big.

All of this made me realize the need for a book, which would need to accomplish the following:

- Clarify what it truly means to audit with agility (and that it does **not** mean simply performing audit work in sprints) and how to go about doing so.

- Provide auditors with the insights necessary to perform value-driven, integrated, adaptable audits.
- Provide clients with actionable advice on how to improve their next audit experience.
- Teach auditors and clients how to improve their working relationship, resulting in greater value to the organization.

2009	2022
The two presenters represented areas that were historically adversaries: Paul from development and John from operations.	While I represented Internal Audit, my copresenter represented the client.
Paul and John explained how Dev and Ops at Flickr got along and worked together.	My copresenter and I explained how the auditor and the audit client got along and worked together.

**Table 3.1: DevOps 2009 Presentation vs
Auditing 2022 Presentation**

In the pages that follow, we will dive deeper into the key practices of value-driven, integrated, adaptable auditing (or just Auditing with Agility for short). You'll learn about the theory behind these practices and see them in action in practical, relatable examples. Many of these practices can be incorporated immediately, without having to undergo a department-wide or organization-wide transformation. The practices don't always have to be auditor driven. Audit clients and auditors alike can use these practices to help create a better, happier audit experience.

What Is Auditing with Agility?

Auditing with Agility moves beyond strict auditing frameworks and truly empowers teams to add the most value possible through a flexible, customizable approach to auditing. It enables teams to experience the benefits of an efficient and value-added audit, while cultivating and leveraging a strong partnership between clients and auditors.

Goals of Auditing with Agility

The goals of Auditing with Agility include those of traditional waterfall auditing (to help the organization achieve its objectives by providing value through assurance and insights) and Agile Auditing (to increase efficiency in the audit process). In addition to these goals, Auditing with Agility strives to deliver even greater value through prioritizing work based on value to the organization, responding to change, delivering results timely, and focusing on outcomes. We can all agree, regardless of whether you're a client or an auditor, that an audit focused on the processes, products, and risks that are absolutely crucial for the organization to achieve its objectives is more valuable than an audit focused on processes, products, and risks that have relatively little impact on the organization. We can also recognize that real-time feedback is more valuable than stale feedback delivered months after identifying a problem. Finally, I'm confident we can agree that wasting time is . . . well . . . a waste of time and not valuable to anyone. By that logic, it's clear that our organizations need to revolutionize the way they conduct and deliver internal audits. That is the intent of Auditing with Agility.

Three Core Components of Auditing with Agility

Auditing with Agility consists of three core components. By focusing how you work on these three components and your desired outcome instead of on a strict framework, you can be assured of a smooth, helpful, empowering audit instead of a dreaded exercise in bureaucracy.

The three core components are:

- Value-driven auditing
- Integrated auditing
- Adaptable auditing

Let's look at each of these in more detail.

Value-Driven Auditing
To be value-driven, the scope of audit work must be driven by what adds the most value to your organization. Each organization may define value differently. Delivery of value in terms of an audit could be assurance and insights in the areas of greatest risk or greatest opportunity for the organization. To help you determine how your organization and its key stakeholders define value, work with your

organization's key stakeholders to understand what they value and how you can align audit work with that definition of value.

Figure 3.1: The Three Core Components of Auditing with Agility

Key outcomes associated with value-driven auditing include greater alignment between audit work and the organization's priorities, expedited delivery of value, and elevated awareness and ability to respond to risks.

Chapter 5 details ways to put this principle into practice. As an appetizer, consider this: delivering results in iterations or sprints is a way to deliver value early and often. Decomposing the audit scope into areas of focus and prioritizing these areas of focus lets value drive the audit's scope.

Measuring progress primarily through delivery of value further facilitates and incentivizes value-driven auditing. If your primary measure of progress is delivery of value, then your team will more likely be motivated to deliver value than they would if something else (like the number of audit reports delivered) was the primary measure of progress.

Another way to evolve to more value-driven auditing is through increasing the visibility of audit work. Making invisible work visible helps the team ensure they're working on tasks that create value. Without visibility of all the work each auditor performs, auditors may spend their time on work that does not result in or contribute to value for the client or the organization.

When the work is visible, other team members can question the value of the work to be completed (not in a malicious sense, but in a way that helps educate themselves or to ensure proper investment of the team's time). If the tasks in question do not add value, then the team can pivot to other tasks that do provide value.

This is closely related to constantly optimizing for global goals, which also supports value-driven work. Global goals for the audit assist in achieving the organization's global goals. By continuously evaluating the team's work to ensure it aligns with global goals, you ensure your team's work provides value to the organization.

Integrated Auditing

Prior to the introduction of integrated auditing, audits were focused primarily on a single aspect, such as financial reporting. In 2012, the Institute of Internal Auditors (IIA) published guidance explaining the next evolution in internal auditing (at the time) was integrated auditing. The IIA defined integrated auditing at that time as an audit with greater breadth in coverage beyond a singular aspect. Integrated auditing included multiple aspects of a process, such as financial, operational, compliance, and technology. By moving to this type of integrated audits, organizations experienced "a more effective and efficient audit engagement," "increased relevance" of audit work, "increased coverage, improved reporting and more effective risk assessments and audit planning," as well as a more holistic view of the risk and control environment under review.[3] What the guidance *doesn't* discuss is integrating audit work with the client's work. Without this level of integration, organizations miss out on an opportunity to further increase efficiency and effectiveness. Audits are still viewed as additional, unplanned work, which hinders audit clients from achieving their primary objectives, setting the foundation for a combative or adversarial relationship.

The concept of taking the next leap in the integrated auditing journey is one of the things that sets Auditing with Agility apart from other practices or hot topics in the auditing industry. Here is where we challenge the perceived boundaries that have historically separated auditors from clients and, in some organizations, driven a wedge between these two groups.

If you're looking to take your audit experience to a new level and set yourself apart from your peers, perhaps you'll want to further your integrated auditing progress by looking beyond integration *within* the audit organization to the possibility of integrating with the client and the client's work, while maintaining the required independence. When auditors and clients work together daily, they take a step closer to integrating their work. For example, working together when determining the audit's scope integrates the client into the audit, giving the client a voice and creating stronger buy-in.

In many situations, auditors cannot successfully complete an audit without the client's help. The client provides insights into the processes under review, including the relevant risks. The client also fulfills evidence requests so the auditors can complete their testing. Therefore, it makes more sense for auditors and clients to work together rather than against each other in order to get the most out of an audit.

While I *am* suggesting that auditors and their clients should work closely together and think of themselves as one team during the audit, I'm *not* suggesting that reporting structures change. Auditors still need to maintain independence and objectivity. Balancing increased integration with independence and objectivity is imperative to the success of a more integrated audit. Chapter 9 explores this balance in greater detail.

Integrated auditing, as part of Auditing with Agility, encourages auditors to find ways to integrate audit work with the client's work. For example, if the client conducts daily stand-ups (or other similar meetings with a different frequency), suggest that the audit team join in on those meetings to (1) better understand the client's priorities and daily work and (2) discuss matters related to the audit, such as open requests and quick questions to clarify the auditors' understanding. This reduces audit-related interruptions to the client's work and decreases or eliminates excessive meetings.

Another way of integrating these two historically segregated types of work is through real-time feedback loops. Real-time feedback doesn't wait until a specified time for feedback. Instead, feedback is provided immediately. In theory, this is fairly intuitive and seems easy. In reality, it takes a safe environment to facilitate effective real-time feedback loops. By integrating auditors and the client, an organization can cultivate a safe environment, which facilitates real-time feedback loops. This, in turn, leads to closer working relationships between auditors and clients, thus reinforcing integration between the two groups.

Integrated auditing in this book also means integrating continuous improvement into the audit process. Insights on how to integrate continuous improvement into your audit process by reflecting on how to become more effective and adjusting behavior accordingly are further explored in Chapter 6.

Adaptable Auditing

Adaptable auditing focuses on improving the ability to respond to change and adding flexibility into the audit process. It is a mindset and a way of working rather than a framework to implement. If your organization has prioritized increasing delivery of value through incorporating adaptability into audit work, you're in luck! What's even better is if your organization hasn't mandated a specific methodology (e.g., Agile Auditing) to achieve this goal.* If this is the case, you have the

---

* Auditing with Agility is not a specific methodology; rather, it is a way of working that empowers auditors and clients to customize audit approaches to best fit each unique situation.

flexibility to be truly agile in your approach to Auditing with Agility. (And this book provides you with the knowledge you need to bring that to life!)

Chapter 7 includes a number of practices you can use to incorporate adaptable auditing. Many of them are derived from the Agile principles of software development, which I've translated into principles of Auditing with Agility. If you're interested in learning more about the Agile Principles, check out the Appendix.

Leveraging self-organizing teams, which encourages high-levels of collaboration, is a way to add adaptability to auditing. In the context of an audit, strong collaboration may look like all of the auditors attending working sessions or walk-throughs, regardless of the control test they're currently working on. This way of working disseminates and shares knowledge among the team members, which better positions the team to pivot when a change is necessary. For example, if a team member is unexpectedly out of the office or unable to complete work on the audit, their teammates can pick up the work left behind without the need for a knowledge-transfer session.

Another principle of adaptable auditing is to embrace changes, even if they occur late in the audit process. If something during the course of the audit necessitates change, the auditor's ability to change course accordingly is imperative. Looking at this from a different perspective, failing to change course when necessary may reduce the value of audit results.

During the onset of the COVID-19 pandemic, my team was performing audits in two key areas that were heavily involved in the organization's response to the pandemic. (To be fair, nearly every part of the organization was impacted in one way or another by the pandemic. Some parts were more involved in driving the organization's response to the pandemic and others proactively took measures to ensure the organization's success in its response. The two areas under review during the audit were examples of the latter.) Had we continued to conduct these audits without pausing to consider a change to our scope or approach, we would have impeded the organization's successful response to the pandemic. Instead, we briefly paused, listened to our clients to understand how they were impacted, including the impact to their availability, and changed our approach accordingly. We continued conducting the audits, but we proceeded with additional empathy for our clients and increased flexibility when scheduling meetings or requesting information. We found ways to fulfill requests on our own and become as efficient as possible with our clients' time. Doing so enabled us to continue to provide assurance in these areas that were now more in the spotlight than ever before, without getting in our clients' way.

Some of the practices within the Agile Auditing framework align with adaptable auditing. Stand-ups, for example, enable audit teams to shift available resources to tasks that need attention and to change testing procedures as needed to reflect the latest information the audit team has. Further, limiting work in process creates the capability (or paves the way) for teams to move with velocity and change course when necessary. When work is in process, it is more difficult to change course or transfer the work to someone else. By limiting work in process, there are small breaks in the work between when one item is completed and another begins. These breaks create natural opportunities to assess the audit's direction and determine if the team needs to change course.

Benefits of Auditing with Agility

At its core, leveraging Auditing with Agility better positions your organization to achieve its objectives. Auditing with Agility also yields additional benefits, including the following outcomes:

- Stronger relationships between auditors and clients
- Increased employee engagement
- Delivery of value focused in areas of greatest risk and highest value to your organization
- Greater buy-in (from both clients and auditors)
- Increased ability to respond to change
- More timely communication of results (and value) to stakeholders
- Elevated awareness of and ability to address risk
- Reduction in time wasted

Let's investigate some of these potential outcomes in detail.

CASE STUDY International Retail Chain: Walmart

As the complexity of Walmart's business and risk profile increased over the years (e.g., expanding into grocery sales, cultivating an international presence, and adding eCommerce capabilities), the organization's Internal Audit team found themselves faced with the need to keep up with the pace of change in order to continue to serve their audit clients. According to Auditboard, Walmart adopted some of the concepts of Auditing with Agility, like iterative delivery, a flexible approach, and prioritizing audit work to focus on the areas of greatest importance. By doing this, Walmart experienced a number of benefits, including:[4]

- Faster resolution of identified gaps/issues through iterative delivery of audit results
- More effective use of resources due to prioritization of work, which enabled realignment of resources with highest priorities
- More engaging relationships with audit customers (the client and other key stakeholders)

Stronger Relationships

Strengthened relationships between clients and auditors is a key benefit of implementing the practices outlined in this book. Without strong relationships between these two groups, clients and auditors can become obstacles for each other, standing in each other's way of achieving goals.

In reality, clients and auditors have been tasked with the same goal: bringing value to the organization and helping it achieve its objectives! By improving the relationship between clients and auditors, clients begin to view auditors as strategic partners instead of adversaries. Because of this, clients consult the auditors sooner and voluntarily, actively seeking out their perspective rather than waiting for the auditors to come to them. This often results in reduced risk to the organization or increased capitalization on opportunities, which helps both the client and auditors achieve their shared goal of helping the organization achieve its objectives.

Think of it this way: instead of working against each other and getting in each other's way, the knowledge you'll gain from this book will help you partner better with each other and work together to achieve your goals. You can not only remove a roadblock but also gain additional support in achieving your goals. That alone should be convincing enough for you to skip ahead to the parts of the book that explain these better ways of working and for you to start implementing them today. But wait . . . there's more. At the risk of selling past the sale, I'll keep going and explain even more benefits.

Increased Employee Engagement

According to Gallup (a global organization focused on improving workplaces that is widely known for assessments, such as the StrengthsFinder assessment and the Q12 engagement survey), "employee engagement is a foundational component to workplace outcomes . . . and engaged employees perform better, which differentiates you from your competitor."[5] Employee engagement is so important to organizations that many of them work with Gallup on a regular basis to assess their employees' level of engagement and identify ways to preserve and enhance engagement.

Increased engagement is an incredibly useful outcome of Auditing with Agility. Auditing with Agility ties directly to a number of Q12 statements in Gallup's engagement survey. To illustrate, I've provided insights on how these better ways of working promote stronger engagement through four of the Q12 statements:[6]

- Q03: At work, I have the opportunity to do what I do best every day.
- Q07: At work, my opinions seem to count.
- Q08: The mission or purpose of my company makes me feel my job is important.
- Q09: My associates or fellow employees are committed to doing quality work.

Q03: At work, I have the opportunity to do what I do best every day

If your skills are not aligned well with the work you do every day, that's pretty disengaging. You may become overwhelmed and struggle just to get through each day. Eventually, you may become discouraged and actively disengaged. On the other hand, if your skills are better aligned with your work and you have the opportunity to leverage your strengths on a daily basis, I imagine you'd be much more engaged and excited about your work.

Self-organizing teams,* a concept used in Auditing with Agility, allow team members to organize around assignments that match their strengths. As such, they provide team members the opportunity to do what they do best each and every day. This leads to more highly engaged team members.

To illustrate with another example, consider the less-collaborative audit approach, where the audit scope is developed in somewhat of a silo with pockets of

---

* See Chapter 7 for more information on self-organizing teams.

input from the client. In this situation, the auditors are tasked with becoming well versed enough in a particular process (or product or service) to assess it.

I explained earlier in this book that auditors are experts in risks and controls and are not necessarily experts in each area that they're auditing. Imagine now that you're an auditor assigned to an audit of an area you're completely unfamiliar with. You're likely to become a bit overwhelmed trying to learn everything you can about this new topic. Now, imagine an audit where you don't have to know everything about the process, product, or service you're auditing. In this instance, you work very closely with the client, who is the expert in the area under review, so you don't need to become the expert. Instead, you can leverage what you're really good at (providing insights on risks and controls) while increasing your knowledge of this new area (without the pressure of being the expert on it). I imagine the second of those two scenarios leaves you much more engaged with your work.

Q07: At work, my opinions seem to count

One of the key behaviors of Auditing with Agility is collaborating with the client, which involves valuing and considering their input. By doing so, auditors show their clients that their opinions truly matter and their input is critical to the audit's success.

Additionally, involving the entire audit team through all key audit activities—such as determining the scope, assigning work, and compiling audit results—shows the audit team that their opinions and input matter as well. In the traditional waterfall approach, staff auditors may not be brought onto the audit until the scope has been identified. This doesn't allow the staff to provide their input or opinion on what should be audited. Instead, the scope is essentially just handed to them to execute. Another option in the waterfall approach to auditing is for the auditor in charge to assign work to the audit staff, sometimes without knowing what tasks the staff would like to work on or what tasks best leverage those auditors' strengths. Neither of these methods value the auditing team members' opinions. Conversely, with Auditing with Agility, audit staff are empowered to provide their input in both scope decisions and assignments, thus reinforcing to them that their opinions count, which builds stronger engagement.

Q08: The mission or purpose of my company makes me feel my job is important

Because Internal Audit is not on the front lines selling the organization's products or services as part of their daily work, it's easy for them to get disconnected from the company's mission and purpose. This can cause auditors to fail to see the value in their own work, which can foster disengagement. The client too may not know how their time spent on an audit ties back to the company's mission or purpose. When the client spends a significant portion of their time working on an audit without a clear connection to the company's organizational goals, they may also lose sight of why they're doing what they do. This could cause the client to feel that their job is less important or their time is less valuable. Behaviors aligned with the *value-driven* element of Auditing with Agility regularly tie audit work to the organization's objectives. This helps support stronger engagement for both auditors and the client. Clearly connecting the time spent on an audit with the company's purpose and articulating how the time invested during the audit is important and supports the company's mission, as is a common practice with value-driven auditing, helps drive higher levels of engagement for all involved.

Q09: My associates or fellow employees are committed to doing quality work

High levels of collaboration between auditors and audit clients make it easier to see what each team member does every day to help your organization achieve its objectives. Rather than viewing each other as adversaries (the client versus the auditors) or competition (auditor versus auditor) and focusing on each other's faults, team members quickly grow to appreciate each other's dedication to their work. By collaborating closely with the client during an audit, auditors gain a unique perspective of the client's daily work, the knowledge and experience the client brings to the job, and the passion the client has for doing their work well. Similarly, because the client works closely with their auditors using this highly collaborative audit approach, the client can see the audit team's commitment to performing quality audit work and helping the organization achieve its objectives. This can preserve or improve employee engagement for both the client and auditors.

The benefits to engagement don't end with the deeper appreciation clients and auditors gain for each other. These better ways of working also facilitate a greater appreciation within the audit team as well. Instead of working primarily independent of each other, as is common when conducting traditional waterfall-style audits, the audit team members work together to complete the audit work.

Because of this, each auditor has an opportunity to help their teammates complete their work and, while doing so, to learn more about the process under review and appreciate their coworkers' skills. I've witnessed this in practice many times, and some of the things I've heard my team members say to to each other to commend their commitment to doing quality work are generalized below:

- "Wow, I didn't realize the control you're testing was so complex!"
- "You really asked great questions during that working session."
- "You really have a gift of discerning through the details and picking out the key risks and controls. I learned a lot from you and will start incorporating what I learned to my own work going forward."

The high levels of collaboration associated with Auditing with Agility can increase employee engagement by making visible others' commitment to doing quality work. The practices in this book also contribute to increased engagement by aligning strengths with assignments, highlighting the importance of the work performed, and empowering associates to provide their input and opinions to create better outcomes for the organization.

Greater Buy-In (from Both the Client and Auditors)

Another potential outcome of Auditing with Agility is *greater buy-in*. When high levels of collaboration and psychological safety are present, as they are when Auditing with Agility, people involved with the audit feel heard. When people feel heard and know that their input has truly been considered, they're more likely to buy into and support the audit and the audit results. With these improved ways of working, the audit is not happening *to* the client; rather, it is happening *with* the client. Both the client and audit staff buy into the audit's scope because they provided their input during the scoping process. They participated in the decision-making process to determine what to include and exclude. Even though the auditors ultimately decide the scope, the client knows that the auditors made a well-informed and thought-out decision, considering input and feedback from the client.

The audit staff also feels more connected to the audit scope. Instead of the auditor in charge handing the scope to them, the staff help determine the scope and therefore have a better understanding of the importance of the items included. This results in the audit staff buying into the scope as well.

This benefit isn't limited to the audit scope. It shows up throughout the audit, particularly when it comes to the client's buy-in on audit observations. Because auditors are integrated into the client's daily work and the client is integrated into the daily audit work, both parties fully understand the importance of the audit observations (everyone buys into the scope, agreeing that the in-scope items are a priority to the organization) and how the conclusion is reached. In my experience, when working in this way, it's typically the client explaining to their leaders why the audit observation is truly a control gap and contending that the audit observation is accurately represented in the audit report. Instead of the auditors trying to convince the client's leaders of the audit observation's accuracy and relevance (which isn't uncommon in audits performed without leveraging the concepts in this book), the client often does the convincing because they buy into and support the audit observation. In some instances where collaboration between auditors and the client is especially strong, the client even helps to identify the audit observation, making it that much easier for them to partner with the auditors to gain support from the client's leaders for the audit observation.

Increased Ability to Respond to Change

In today's constantly changing environment, risks change faster than ever before. Organizations must adapt to the rapidly changing environment and risks to thrive or even survive. Auditors must respond to changes as well. Those who don't will quickly find themselves obsolete. Auditing with Agility provides auditors the tools necessary to respond to change (e.g., retrospective reviews and periodic reassessments of the audit scope, adjusting as needed). *Increasing the ability to respond to change* better positions the organization to achieve its objectives as the audit embraces change, enabling the audit to remain focused on what's most critical to achievement of the organization's objectives.

Less Time Wasted

Reducing the amount of time wasted is one of the simplest yet potentially one of the most rewarding outcomes of adopting the practices in this book. Investing a significant amount of time into something just to find out you wasted your time is incredibly frustrating and can be quite disengaging. That's why this benefit, reducing the amount of time wasted during an audit, may be the benefit you most enjoy. Simple practices can enable your team to reap this benefit rather quickly. For example, reducing multitasking is a straightforward practice that drastically reduces wasted time by limiting context switching. Additionally, the intentionally increased collaboration between the client and auditors, paired with stronger alignment between audit work and business value, paves the way for audit results with a clear value proposition to stakeholders. That clear value proposition reduces the likelihood that auditors, the client, or executive leaders view the audit as a non-value-added activity (also referred to as a waste of time).

Additional Benefits

The intent of this chapter is not to provide an exhaustive list of the possible outcomes and benefits associated with Auditing with Agility. Instead, the intent is to share some of the possible outcomes you can experience through these better ways of working.

In addition to those benefits listed above, organizations leveraging Auditing with Agility can also experience delivery of greater value and communication of results (and thus delivery of that greater value) sooner, which creates an elevated awareness of and ability to address risks.

Auditing with Agility focuses efforts on the organization's highest priorities, opportunities, and risks. When auditors focus on areas that are *not* a high priority for the organization, that *don't* present substantial opportunities for the organization, or that *don't* pose a significant risk to achieving the organization's objectives, the auditors deliver minimal value. On the other hand, when auditors focus their efforts on the areas of highest priority to the organization, areas that present the greatest opportunity for organizations to improve or succeed, and the outcomes most desired by the organization's stakeholders, then the auditors deliver exponentially more value to the organization.

A common outcome of Auditing with Agility is *delivery of results (and thus value) sooner* than when performing an audit without leveraging these practices. By communicating results sooner, organizations also experience *elevated awareness of and ability to address risk exposures*. When audit results are delivered earlier, stakeholders become aware of the associated risk exposure sooner, and the client can address identified control gaps sooner. Those control gaps present risks that could prevent your organization from achieving its objectives, so when the client addresses them sooner, your organization is better positioned to fulfill its mission. Organizations can't fix gaps they're not aware of. On the other hand, organizations could also over-control a risk. If they're not aware of redundant efforts to manage a risk, they can't fix that either. With their fresh, objective perspective, auditors focused on the most relevant risks to the organization—who integrate their work with their clients to gain a deeper understanding of the area under review without distracting their clients from their daily work and who can pivot as needed to stay focused on emerging risks (i.e., those who audit with agility)—can identify those situations where the organization redundantly manages a risk.

Furthermore, using these techniques, the audit scope will be more closely and clearly aligned with the most significant risks your organization currently faces, those that pose the greatest risk to achieving the organization's objectives. Because of this, the results communicated in the audit report provide value tied directly to the organization's objectives, regardless of whether the report articulates control gaps, offers assurance that key controls are designed and operating effectively, or both. This knowledge helps the client and your organization's other key stakeholders pursue organizational goals. Elevated awareness of how well risks are managed increases the organization's ability to better manage those risks.

The potential outcomes presented here are foundational in nature. The benefits you experience when implementing the solutions outlined in the next section of this book may include some beyond those outlined in this section.

The Smorgasbord (or À La Carte Menu) of Options

Auditing with Agility is not a framework. It is designed like a menu of à la carte items or a smorgasbord, where you can see all the options and select the ones that best align with your needs or wants. Do you want a well-balanced meal? Great! You'll choose some grilled chicken breast, steamed broccoli, and jasmine rice. Need to load up on carbs? Grab some dinner rolls (don't forget the butter), pasta, and a bit of fruit. Want to satisfy your sweet tooth? Head straight to the dessert section and put some chocolate cake and ice cream on your plate.

Instead of food, Auditing with Agility is a smorgasbord of practices and ways of working from which you select and compile a meal (or in this case, an approach for the audit) based on each individual audit's needs and desired outcomes. When approaching an audit, consider a number of factors (e.g., both the auditors' needs and the client's, the complexity of the area under review, the team's willingness to experiment with different ways of working) and what outcomes you'd like to achieve. Then select the specific concepts in each of the core principles of Auditing with Agility (value-driven auditing, integrated auditing, and adaptable auditing) that make the most sense for that particular audit.

Chapters 5 through 7 dive deep into the practices and principles of the three core components: value-driven auditing, integrated auditing, and adaptable auditing. Think of each of these chapters as sections of the smorgasbord. For every audit, you'll select an element (or more) from each of the three core components of Auditing with Agility to build a customized approach for that audit.

For example, perhaps your next audit is with a team you've audited before. The last time you worked with this team, the reporting phase was littered with ongoing negotiations. This time around, you want to deliver results sooner and build strong relationships between auditors and audit clients. As you make your way through the Auditing with Agility smorgasbord, you should probably try some *iterative delivery* from Chapter 5, so you can achieve those outcomes by agreeing on results, delivering them, and moving on.

Or perhaps the area you're auditing is a large, complex process that is prone to rapid change. In this instance, you're targeting the outcomes of better alignment of audit activities with the most relevant and emerging risks, even as they evolve and increased ability to respond to change. Go ahead and put *prioritized areas of focus* from Chapter 5 and *intentional pauses to reevaluate priority* from Chapter 7 on your plate.

Is the audit team frustrated from the last audit, when both the client and auditors suffered from ineffective communications about the documentation requested? Do you want to improve collaboration and waste less time on this next audit? Sounds like you could use an *intentionally collaborative planning approach* from Chapter 6, which integrates the client into the creation of the document request list.

Have the audit team members shared that their assigned tasks on the last audit didn't really align with their development goals? Sounds like you want to improve alignment between assignments and team members' interests and goals to accelerate your team's learning and growth. Top your plate off with *self-organizing teams* from Chapter 7.

What about the next audit? Grab a clean plate and go back to the Auditing with Agility smorgasbord to pick out the elements needed to create a customized approach for that specific audit.

If you're an auditor reading this book, I know the burning question in your mind is "What about IIA Standards? Auditors still need to comply with them." You're absolutely right. Auditing with Agility enables you to achieve a number of benefits *while still complying with the IIA's Standards*! That's the short answer. We get into the details (the "verify" part to satisfy your need to "trust but verify") in Chapter 9.

ADVENTURES IN AUDITING
Auditing with Agility at a Fortune 100 Company

In 2021, I started a biennial audit for the IAM team at a Fortune 100 company. When it was time to think about how we would conduct this audit, we looked to some of the past lessons we had learned—namely, that we couldn't just copy and paste the same auditing framework we had used successfully in the past. Something I realized over my past two years of experiments with Agile Auditing is that one size does not fit all. Instead, we took a different approach: Auditing with Agility. We knew that if we focused on the three key components (value-driven, integrated, and adaptable), then we could craft the right auditing experience for this team.

First, we delivered our audit in thirty-day sprints because the IAM team already used such a schedule. We integrated with their style of working instead of imposing a new way of working onto them and creating friction and impediments. Second, we came together as one team, not auditors and audit clients separately. We collectively crafted the scope of the audit so that it best met the needs of the organization. Third, we built in a mindset of continual learning and experimentation from day one. We also utilized making work visible, self-organizing teams, and greater collaboration. In this audit, compared to our audit of the same space in 2019, we were able to achieve the following results:

- We got faster: days spent auditing were reduced by 10.5% and the speed of delivery increased by 48.7%.
- Delivering sooner meant the IAM team could actually show progress by the final audit report.
- We also got better: we were able to cover more areas than in 2019, and satisfaction between the two teams increased by two levels.

Conclusion

As you've seen in this chapter, to truly reap the benefits promised by Agile Auditing, we must move beyond a strict framework and focus on *being* agile instead of "doing Agile." When we make this change, we experience the benefits we sought in the first place—more effective response to change, increased efficiency, communication of results sooner, stronger alignment and engagement between teams, and increased delivery of real value. In the next chapter, I'll break down these benefits even further by exploring several of the key problems that waterfall auditing creates in today's environment and how practicing Auditing with Agility can solve those problems.

Chapter 4

Internal Auditing Problems
and Solutions

As we explored earlier, traditional waterfall auditing presents challenges in today's world. Auditing with Agility provides solutions for these challenges, including the challenge of an adversarial relationship that often results between clients and auditors. This chapter explores those problems and introduces solutions from an Auditing with Agility mindset, first exploring problems the client often experiences, then taking a look at problems auditors encounter. These problems lead to strained, adversarial relationships between clients and auditors, as well as inefficiencies and decreased effectiveness. Concepts introduced in this section to resolve the specific problems are part of the Auditing with Agility smorgasbord. Subsequent chapters expand upon each of the solutions.

Problems and Introduction to Solutions:
The Client's Side

When the auditors come knocking, if you're part of the team being audited, you might wish you could run and hide. Or maybe you wish you could use a Jedi mind trick and convince the auditors this isn't the process they're looking for. Unfortunately, neither of those are likely to be successful solutions. Before digging into the solutions, let's first gain a better understanding of the problems at the root of this behavior or fear. If you're an auditor, please don't skip this section, as it will give you a perspective you may not have previously considered. A little bit of empathy and perspective-taking can really help to resolve conflicts.

Audit Work Is Unplanned Work

Problem

Picture this: you're a software developer, and you've got your work all planned out for the week, month, or whatever interval you use to plan and prioritize work. All is going well until the auditors show up and add more work to your plate. Basically, you have three choices: fail to deliver your own work that you've prioritized, ignore the audit work that has been added to your plate, or work ridiculous hours to meet both commitments. Let's eliminate the third option right away. Working a ton of hours is neither sustainable nor engaging. So you're down to two options, creating a lose-lose situation. What if there was a fourth option that could get you a win? What if you knew ahead of time how the audit would impact your workload?

Solution

With Auditing with Agility, you can reduce the unplanned work brought on by an audit. With the better ways of working outlined in this book, auditors and their clients work closely together throughout the entire audit process. There are no surprises, and that also means no surprises when it comes to the work necessary to complete the audit work. If you're heavily involved in discussions to determine the scope of the audit, you will have a better idea which of your team members will be spending time working on the audit. Therefore, you will be better able to plan your team's workload to accommodate the audit work alongside your team's nonaudit work. If you have an intake process to help turn unplanned work into planned work, encourage your auditors to use that process. While they may not know the specific documentation requests they'll submit when they start the audit, they can still leverage your intake process to help you plan for the impact of the audit on your team's workload.

For example, I worked with a client who used an intake form to generate a task card and place that task card in the team's backlog or schedule it alongside their other assignments. This enabled the client to plan for the incoming audit work and account for it in weekly sprint planning sessions (where the client planned out the work they could commit to each week). Because of this, my client could adjust their team's commitments to account for the audit work, reducing the need to miss deadlines or give up the dream of a work-life balance to work unreasonable hours during the audit.

This is one example of integrating audit work into your daily work. The sections of this book that follow introduce other techniques to better integrate audit work into your daily work and turn the unplanned work into planned work. How great is that?! Besides, nobody likes surprises from their auditors (unless that surprise is a box of your favorite donuts and fresh coffee from your favorite coffee shop). Either way (coffee and donuts, or the implementation of the practices outlined in this book), you're going to have a much more enjoyable audit experience.

Auditors Don't Understand Our Business

Problem

How frustrating is it to go through an audit when the auditors don't have a deep enough understanding of your area? That frustration is likely compounded because this lack of understanding might lead the auditors to focus on things that are not important to you. This in turn means you spend a bunch of time answering questions that are irrelevant to your team's mission and digging up useless documentation for the auditors to review. If that isn't a waste of time, I don't know what is. It's no wonder you're not excited when those darn auditors show up. Why don't they just become experts in the areas they're auditing?

Solution

Perspective-taking might be helpful here. How much time do you spend with your auditors each year? It's likely somewhere around three months every other year (on a part-time basis, since they're typically on three or more audits at once, and you're not spending 100% of your time during those three months on the audit or with the auditors). If that's the case, your auditors spend time auditing at least twelve areas each year, and not every area is audited every year; some go a few years between audits. Is it reasonable to expect auditors to be experts in every area they audit? Realistically, no. It is, however, reasonable to expect your auditors to be experts in risks and controls. Combine that with the expertise that you and your team bring to the table, and you've got something equivalent to the A-Team. Everyone brings unique strengths, skills, and expertise to the team that, in isolation, may not be particularly useful. But combine those diverse attributes, and you've got a team that can really add value!

Instead of expecting the auditors to have complete expertise in your processes and business area, let them leverage yours. Help them understand what your team is charged with achieving. Explain to them why certain things you do are more important than others. Show them how you make sure your team is positioned to accomplish its objectives. Tell them what has to go right and what can't go wrong for you to be successful. Share onboarding materials (what would you provide a new hire on your team to get up to speed quickly?) or fundamental training courses with your auditors to help them understand your particular product or service. Bear in mind that the auditors will possess a certain baseline level of knowledge to perform the audit with proficiency and due professional care, as required by IIA Standards; however, they are not required to bring complete and total expertise of the area under review. Investing your time in helping your auditors understand what they need to know about your part of the organization will be time well spent. Not only will you strengthen your relationship with your auditors (and learn how to leverage them to your advantage when you need expertise on risks and controls), but you'll also get more value out of the audit because it will be more heavily focused on the areas of most importance to you and your team.

Audit Reports Don't Tell Us Anything We Don't Already Know

Problem

Another complaint auditors sometimes receive from the client is that the audit report told the client what they already knew and didn't tell them anything new. The client didn't find value in the audit work, so they viewed the audit as a waste of time. This is precisely the opposite of what we're all going for. Audits should add value to an organization, not waste time! If you had a magic wand and could use it to change the audit to make it more useful, what would it look like? Would it focus on the areas most important to your team? Would the report tell you whether the controls you most depend on are working like you think they are or expect that they are? What if the audit provided recommendations on ways to improve your work by eliminating duplicative controls? What if it shared ideas on how to automate manual, repetitive processes so you could focus on levering your strengths for something more valuable? What if it provided insights on how your own team could leverage better ways of working to achieve your desired outcomes?

Solution

As a member of the auditor community, I'm here to tell you that's what we want too. We truly aren't here to spend our time (and yours) doing a bunch of work all just to hand you a report that doesn't help you or provide valuable insights. The solution here is working *with* your auditors so they can create a valuable audit and deliver valuable audit results.

Okay, so we're aligned on what we both want: value-added work and insights that are actionable and useful. But how do we get there? The answer is through Auditing with Agility. Through the techniques outlined in the upcoming sections of this book, such as putting value in the driver's seat, integrating Internal Audit and the client throughout the audit process, and adapting to change, you can help educate your auditors about the risks you're most concerned about and the controls you depend on the most. Then, when the auditors deliver the audit results, they'll be focused on the areas most important to the success of your team and organization. There you have it! And you don't need a magic wand to do it. This book equips you with the knowledge you need to leverage your audit friends to help you achieve your objectives.

Problems and Introduction to Solutions: The Auditor's Side

The client is not alone in experiencing problems during an audit. Auditors have their own set of problems to deal with during audits. Auditors, read on to explore some of these problems. I bet you can relate to some, if not all of them. If you're an audit client, I have the same ask of you that I had of the auditors in the previous section: Please don't skip this section. By understanding the challenges your auditors face, you'll be better positioned to help them create solutions that will ultimately benefit you as well.

Context Switching

Problem

When you stop doing one task and move to another, that's context switching. Your brain has to switch from thinking about the context of the task you just stopped and switch to the context of the task you are starting or picking back up. This increases mental load and leads to inefficiencies (aka wasted or lost time). When you stop doing one task, move to another, then stop that task to move back to the original task (or take on yet another task), that's a lot more context switching.

Gerald Weinberg, author of *Quality Software Management: Systems Thinking* provides the following rule of thumb with regard to context switching, based on his observations: the more tasks you have going on at once, the more inefficient you are.[1] If you focus on one task at a time, 100% of your time is dedicated to that task, resulting in no time lost switching between tasks (i.e., no time lost to context switching). Adding just one additional task reduces the amount of time you're focusing on your actual work and increases the amount of time wasted due to context switching. Table 4.1 shows how inefficiencies increase dramatically as you take on more tasks at once.

Studies have confirmed the inefficiency of context switching. For example, Gallup conducted an interview with Gloria Mark, PhD. and Associate Professor at the University of California, Irvine, on the subject of context switching. According to Dr. Mark's study, once interrupted, it takes you an average of twenty-three minutes and fifteen seconds to get "back to the task you were doing before you were interrupted."[2]

Number of Simultaneous Projects	Percent of Working Time Available per Project	Time Lost to Context Switching
1	100%	0%
2	40%	20%
3	20%	40%
4	10%	60%
5	5%	75%

Table 4.1: Waste Caused by Project Switching
Reproduced from Weinberg, Gerald M. *Quality Software Management: Systems Thinking.* Dorset House, New York: 1992.

In an audit, context switching looks like this: Auditors have multiple control tests in process concurrently and are working on about four audits at the same time as well. Not only are they using a lot of mental capacity to switch from one control to another, but they're also juggling multiple different audits too! There's a good chance those audits focus on very different subjects as well.

Here's how a typical day in the life of an auditor may look. The auditor's day starts out with a meeting to understand how access reviews are performed for the payroll system for the payroll audit. Next, the auditor runs to another meeting to work with the investments team to obtain trade confirmations for a sample of trades to be tested in an investments audit. There's finally a quick break in the day to go back to the access control and evaluate the control's design, using what the auditor learned in the first meeting. A little later, the auditor receives evidence related to change approvals for the wire payment system, which was requested two weeks prior. Now that the auditor finally has the requested change approvals, they put down the payroll access review control and start testing the change approvals. Not only has the auditor switched between three different control types (access reviews, trade confirmations, and change approvals), they also switched between three completely different organizational processes (payroll, investments, and cash management). All in just one day, likely all before lunch too!

Solution

A solution to this madness is to limit multitasking. As Jonathan Smart puts it in *Sooner Safer Happier*, "stop starting, start finishing."[3] While it's tempting to get everything started as soon as possible, it's wildly inefficient to do so. Instead, by limiting the number of items that are in process, auditors can limit the time lost to context switching. This reduces the auditor's mental load and will likely result in fewer mistakes and less burnout. It also reduces the amount of transition work needed if the auditor gets pulled off of an audit to work on something else or is out of the office unexpectedly. Instead of having six or more controls in varying stages of completion and scrambling to bring someone else up to speed on all of them, there are likely only a couple of items in progress that will need to be transitioned. Better yet, the auditor is more likely to be able to easily wrap up the few items in process before switching over to the next project.

Note that collaboration between auditors and audit clients better enables limited multitasking. Working closely together, auditors and clients expedite learning, fulfillment of requests, and delivery of results, which reduces the wait time and encourages teams to finish a task before starting a new one.

Managing Chokepoints/Dependencies on Certain People

Problem

At times, auditors identify key person risks, or single points of dependency in the processes they're assessing. But how often do auditors recognize and address those same risks within the audit process itself? More specifically, auditors experience the fallout from relying on an individual to test a control but rarely implement countermeasures. When that person is sick or is pulled off the audit to focus on a different activity, the rest of the team scrambles to pick up the pieces, often making duplicate requests or inquiries of the client to recover the information lost when the originally assigned auditor left abruptly. This not only increases wasted time, both for the auditors and the client, but also doesn't do much to help build a strong relationship with the client. In fact, in many cases, it further strains the already tense relationship between the two teams.

Solution

Countermeasures, such as increasing visibility of the audit team's work and taking a more collaborative approach within the audit team, can help eliminate single points of dependency and reduce the impact of losing a team member. It's also a worthwhile investment in the audit team's development and growth to expand the team's knowledge beyond the specific controls each individual is tasked with testing, giving them a broader understanding of the end-to-end process under review or the entire technology product under review.

Ongoing Observation Negotiations after Agreement

Problem

How many times have you presented an audit observation to your clients, aligned on the details, and then in the next status meeting or in the closing/exit meeting, negotiations began all over again? To be honest, I've lost count myself. I'm pretty sure I don't want to know because it's likely way more wasted time than I'm comfortable admitting.

Solution

The solution here is to deliver results and move on. Delivering audit results iteratively reduces the chances of negotiations continuing after initial alignment on the observation.* Once the key individuals align on the accuracy of the observation and other supporting details, auditors can finalize the audit observation and set the expectation that it can no longer be changed. This is similar to how open audit observations are handled after report issuance: the audit observation stands and can be closed once remediation of the gap is validated, but the details of the documented gap remain. Then everyone can move on to what's next. As with any cultural change, it's important to over-communicate this to all involved parties. When you think you've communicated it sufficiently, keep communicating—you're probably only halfway there.

---

* An observation in an audit is defined by the IIA as "any identified and validated gap between the current and desired state arising from an assurance engagement."[4]

There are many ways to deliver iteratively in the context of an audit. One way is to borrow techniques from Scrum or Agile Auditing and break the audit timeline down into sprints, delivering in consistent and predictable time-based intervals. Another method is to finalize and communicate results based on a trigger point other than at specific time-based intervals. Regardless of the technique you use, work together to finalize the results and then move on.

Conclusion

These are just a sample of some of the problems both the client and auditors face during audits. By reading through both of these sections, you know more about the challenges both clients and auditors encounter, and perhaps you realize you have more in common than you may have originally thought. You also got a glimpse of how the upcoming sections in this book can help you and your partners in other parts of the organization solve those problems. We'll dive deeper into those solutions (and many more) next.

As we covered in Chapter 3, Auditing with Agility is like a smorgasbord of options from which you select, creating a customized approach tailored to meet your organization's unique needs during an audit. One way to select the elements to incorporate on a given audit is to select based on problems you're facing. If you've been struggling with audit work as unplanned work, why not try a highly collaborative planning approach or a shared task board between the client and auditors? Are the auditors burned out from too much context switching? I'd recommend you try limiting multitasking. If you aren't looking for solutions to specific problems or challenges, don't worry; Auditing with Agility is still for you. In the next part of this book, we'll explore each component (value-driven auditing, integrated auditing, and adaptable auditing) and practices for you to use to enhance the audit experience at your organization and achieve desired outcomes. By doing so, you will better position your organization to achieve its objectives, while enjoying less painful and more valuable audits.

The Three Core
Components of
Auditing with Agility

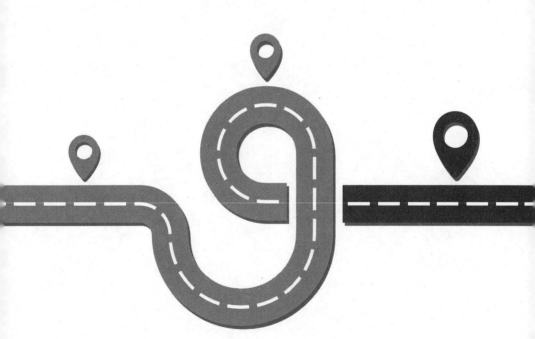

The narrative of my journey in Part I was an appetizer introducing you to some of the practices, behaviors, and benefits associated with Auditing with Agility. In Chapter 4, you dug a little deeper into the problems you may face in an audit, regardless of whether you represent the client or the auditors (think of it like the salad or the second course in a multicourse meal).

Now, here we are at the main course. It's time to closely examine the solutions introduced in the previous sections. As you navigate this section, you'll gain a deeper understanding of key concepts used in Auditing with Agility. This section is organized by the three core elements of Auditing with Agility: value-driven auditing, integrated auditing, and adaptable auditing.

Many of the practices I describe in the following chapters support more than one of the three key components of Auditing with Agility. Those practices are introduced in the chapter that corresponds with the core component most closely aligned with the practice; however, it's important to keep in mind that you can leverage these practices to achieve the goals of more than one core component. For example, standups support all three core components: pursuing simplicity and increasing visibility support both adaptable auditing and value-driven auditing, and constantly optimizing for the global goals and integrated planning both support integrated auditing and value-driven auditing. As you navigate the chapters that follow, focus more on each practice and how you can adopt it to achieve your goals and desired outcomes, while focusing less on a strict alignment between practice and core component.

Value-driven auditing practices and principles:

- Value actionable insights over extensive documentation
- Satisfy stakeholders through the delivery of value
- Deliver value frequently
- Break down the audit scope into manageable pieces
- Measure progress through the delivery of value
- Increase visibility
- Constantly optimize for global goals rather than individual goals

Integrated auditing practices and principles:

- Practice intentional collaboration
- Work together daily
- Work as a single team toward a collective goal
- Use integrated planning
- Create feedback loops

Adaptable auditing practices and principles:

- Value people over processes
- Respond to change over strictly following a plan
- Prefer face-to-face conversation over text-based, asynchronous communication
- Promote sustainable work
- Pursue simplicity
- Leverage self-organizing teams
- Organize stand-ups
- Limit work in process
- Reduce batch sizes

Chapter 5

Practices and Principles of Value-Driven Auditing

In value-driven auditing, the scope of work is driven primarily by what adds the most value to the organization (e.g., areas of greatest risk or greatest opportunity for the organization). Norman Marks suggests asking the following questions to determine value:[1]

- "What could go wrong and adversely affect the achievement of the objective?"
- "What needs to go right for you [or the organization] to succeed?"
- "What opportunities might arise that would enhance success?"

This chapter will take a deeper look at some practices that can support a value-driven audit:

- Value actionable insights over extensive documentation.
- Satisfy stakeholders through the delivery of value.
- Deliver value frequently.
- Break down the audit scope into manageable pieces.
- Measure progress through the delivery of value.
- Increase visibility.
- Constantly optimize for global goals rather than individual goals.

Value Actionable Insights over Extensive Documentation

Borrowed from one of the Agile Values of software development, an important concept of value-driven auditing is valuing actionable insights over extensive documentation. The original Agile value, focused on software development as its primary use case, encourages teams to value working products or software over extensive documentation. This concept doesn't directly relate to or resonate with auditors, since the output of an audit is not working software or a specific product that either works or doesn't work. The output of an audit is assurance or actionable, value-added insights. Therefore, I modified this Agile value to more clearly apply to audit work: *value assurance or actionable insights over extensive documentation.*

Documentation is what auditors' dreams are made of. Value-driven auditing does not require auditors to abandon documentation altogether. We still need documentation to support our work. This means that auditors shouldn't lose focus on the end goal of delivering assurance or actionable insights for the sake of documentation. Value-driven auditors place greater value on delivering results than they do on extensive documentation. Auditors can increase the value they deliver by anchoring back to the profession's overarching goal of providing assurance and insights to stakeholders. It's important to think of "delivering results" in terms of an *outcome*, not an *output*. Placing a great deal of value on delivering an audit report for the sake of delivering an audit report (an output of the audit) isn't going to help the organization much. Instead, delivering value through providing assurance or insights on high or emerging risk areas or increased alignment between audit scope and stakeholder expectations while maintaining independence (outcomes of an audit) helps the organization far more.

To expand on this, let's explore an example. Workpapers are important to the audit process, as they provide support for the conclusions reached and the results communicated in an audit report. While workpapers are important, they are only visible to the auditors and those groups who audit the auditors. The audience is limited.

On the flip side, audit reports have a much larger audience, often both internal and external to the organization, and have a greater impact. Value-driven auditors don't spend their time dotting their i's and crossing their t's in workpapers; rather, they redirect those efforts to deliverables that have a larger audience and greater impact: the audit report. Workpapers are still documented, just perhaps not always with perfect grammar. This aligns with Auditing with Agility's intended outcome of less time wasted.

Satisfy Stakeholders through Delivery of Value

Another key concept of value-driven auditing is to prioritize stakeholder satisfaction through delivery of value (i.e., delivery of audit work that is aligned with what's most important to the organization). Understanding early in the audit process what key stakeholders, including the clients, value most is key to successfully delivering value and stakeholder satisfaction.

Stakeholders vary from one organization to another; however, they typically include the board of directors (or the audit committee of the board) and the organization's senior executives. Stakeholders can also include other parties, such as frontline leaders accountable for the organization's operations and technology product owners. Regardless of who the organization's key stakeholders are, they will value audit work that is focused on the highest, most relevant risks and the areas that are important to achieving the organization's objectives.

But wait, doesn't this go against an auditor's obligation to remain independent of the client? Yes, but only if the auditors impair their independence and objectivity and act on *behalf* of the client. That's not what this principle is asking you to do.

This principle is suggesting that auditors consider what stakeholders value when performing audits. It doesn't say to take orders from the client or to let the client decide what gets audited and what doesn't. It suggests that auditors can increase the value they add to their organization by understanding stakeholder needs and considering them when identifying the audit scope, testing controls within the audit's scope, and communicating results of the audit.

Perhaps the client of one area really values the services provided by a third party and depends heavily on that third-party service provider for the success of the process or product for which they're accountable. In an audit of this area, the auditors should consider this high level of dependency on that third-party service provider when determining what to audit. The auditors should not let the client determine the scope of the audit; rather, they should consider input from the client when making audit decisions. By considering the client's needs when determining what to audit, auditors create more buy-in from their clients.

In an audit of a different area within the organization, perhaps the client isn't specifically concerned with a particular set of controls because they believe the controls to be effective. If these are key controls, upon which the success of the process or product depends, the auditors consider the client's input with regard to these controls; however, they should probably still include the controls in the audit's scope due to the importance of those controls in ensuring the organization can achieve its objectives. In this situation, the auditors still prioritized value for key stakeholders, as the effectiveness of those controls drive value to the organization. Inclusion of those controls in the audit's scope will result in either independent confirmation to the client that those key controls are indeed effective (value for the client) or that those controls are not operating as effectively as the client thought (also value for the client). Either way, value is delivered to the organization's key stakeholders because the audit work is focused on the areas most important to the success of the area under review.

> **Note for clients:** Help your auditors understand what delivery of value looks like to you. What's most important to your process or product? What are you worried about? What controls really need to be effective for your team to achieve their objectives? Where do you need help improving how you do what you do? What controls seem to take more time and documentation than necessary that would be helpful to get the auditors' perspective on better ways to manage the associated risk? Auditors can certainly make educated guesses about what value they should deliver, but they're more likely to get it precisely aligned with your definition of value if you collaborate with them during that determination.

Deliver Value Frequently

Another element of value-driven auditing is to deliver value early and often, instead of only at the end of a months-long audit. This results in the following potential outcomes: more timely communication of results and value, elevated awareness of risks, increased ability to address control gaps, and amplified ability to respond to change.

Value-driven auditors communicate and finalize audit results as soon as they're identified. Working in this manner enables the client to address audit observations, including control gaps, unmitigated risks, and underutilized opportunities, sooner, preferably before the gaps turn into realized risks with actual losses. This better positions the organization to achieve its objectives.

To illustrate, consider the traditional waterfall audit approach, where the reporting stage follows fieldwork (the stage of the audit where testing occurs). Final results are not communicated to the client until the reporting stage, which could be months after the results were identified, especially if an audit observation (or assurance that a control was designed or operating effectively) was identified at the beginning of the fieldwork stage.

Now consider an audit performed with a focus on early and continuous delivery of value. Here, the auditors communicate results of a specific control test to the client when they finish testing that control rather than waiting until all control tests are complete. While the auditors move their focus to the next control or grouping of controls to test, the client can begin addressing any audit observations the auditors shared with them. Audits performed in this way get that value into the client's hands sooner, which means they can swiftly improve their processes and reduce risk, impressing their stakeholders. In other words, delivering results frequently often allows clients to pivot their work as needed to respond to change sooner. If a key control is not effective and the auditors communicate this to their client earlier in the process, the client can shift its focus to fixing that control gap sooner. That is, by delivering value frequently, auditors increase their client's ability to respond to change.

There are a few ways you can deliver audit results frequently. Two common ways are *delivering iteratively* and *delivering in sprints*. Some use these terms interchangeably. In this book, *sprints* and *iterations* have distinct implications. Sprints are consistently defined timeboxes. That is to say that when an audit is delivered in X number of sprints, each of those X sprints lasts the same amount of time (e.g., two weeks). Teams also use iterations to deliver value throughout an audit rather than waiting until the end; however, with iterations, the triggers for delivery are more flexible and aren't always tied to a strict and consistent timebox. Because sprints are a way to deliver iteratively, sprints are a *type* of iteration.

Iterative Delivery

Delivering iteratively provides a bit more freedom than only delivering in sprints. Auditors deliver results based on certain triggers. Those triggers can be anything. A few examples are identifying a risk or flawed control and completing a specific portion of the work.

Let's explore an example of that second option, reporting results once a specific portion of the work is complete. Imagine you're working on an audit as an auditor. This audit's scope covers three key processes: acquisition, maintenance, and retirement of assets. You've completed the audit work on the acquisition process, but perhaps the work on the maintenance and retirement processes aren't yet complete. Go ahead and finalize and deliver those results associated with the acquisition process so the client can start addressing them. Once you're finished with another process or the rest of the audit, you can deliver the remaining results too. Essentially, why wait to package all the value up together and wait until the end to deliver it? Isn't it better to let the client start addressing observations as soon as possible?

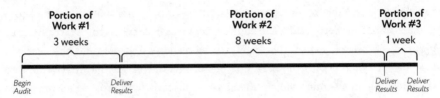

| Portion of Work #1 | Portion of Work #2 | Portion of Work #3 |
| 3 weeks | 8 weeks | 1 week |

Begin Audit   Deliver Results   Deliver Results   Deliver Results

Figure 5.1: Audit Delivered in Iterations Aligned with Specific Portions of Work

Sprints

Sprints are timeboxes and are the key delivery model of Agile Auditing. As previously explored, the strict, one-size-fits-all nature of how organizations often mandate use of Agile Auditing creates challenges, such as resistance to change and lack of clarity around the goal of Agile Auditing. That being said, organizations applying Agile Auditing practices, such as sprint-based audit delivery, without the strict mandate and blind application of the concept in every situation can audit with agility and help their organizations succeed.

In conversations with audit practitioners from multiple organizations and multiple industries, I learned that teams often confuse sprints with divisions of work or areas of focus (e.g., pieces of the audit scope). While sprints may line up well with tidy divisions of audit scope (cover scope area X in sprint 1 and scope area Y in sprint 2), there isn't always a one-for-one alignment between sprints and scope areas.

The key differentiator here is that sprints break down the audit's *timeline* into manageable pieces, not the scope (we look at breaking the scope into manageable pieces in the next section).

Sprints are timeboxes, nothing more, nothing less. Sprints range from one to four weeks and are consistent throughout an audit to ensure predictability of delivery. When delivering in sprints, the client and auditors both know at what intervals results are expected to be delivered. If the team chooses four-week sprints, then the auditors deliver assurance and actionable insights every four weeks. If the team chooses one-week sprints, then the auditors deliver assurance and actionable insights on a weekly basis.

Throughout each sprint, auditors and the client continue to collaborate as the audit progresses. Audit observations are discussed with the client as soon as they are identified to ensure accuracy of the observation and an understanding of the related risk. At the end of the timebox, the sprint is over, and the auditors communicate results to key stakeholders. Any of the work that remains incomplete at the conclusion of the sprint moves into the next sprint.

When the final sprint concludes, the auditors deliver the final set of audit results. In some cases, this may include only the results from the final sprint, since results from prior sprints were previously communicated. In other cases, the communication at the end of the final sprint includes audit observations identified in the final sprint, as well as observations communicated in prior sprints, providing an overarching view of the area under review. Figure 5.2 illustrates an audit delivered in three four-week sprints, totalling a three month time frame.

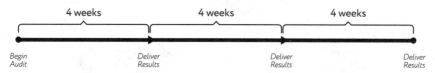

Figure 5.2: Audit Delivered in Sprints

Compare this to the delivery schedule of a waterfall audit, as seen below.

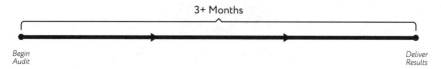

Figure 5.3: Waterfall Delivery of an Audit

Under the sprint-based approach, the auditors may deliver a final report at the end of the audit that includes all of the observations identified throughout the audit, even those that were previously communicated to the client through the earlier iterations.

How to Deliver in Sprints

So how do you go about delivering an audit in sprints? First, you need to figure out the timeboxes. How frequently do you want to deliver results to the client? There is no right or wrong answer. In reality, you'll pick a length of time, try it out, figure out whether it worked really well or if another length of time would be better, and adjust accordingly. Generally, the shorter the sprint, the better. Shorter sprints get results into clients' hands sooner.

The key is to deliver results at consistent intervals. If you select two-week sprints for an audit, stick with it throughout the audit (unless you learn that it is *really* not working, then anchor back to your goals of delivering value and incorporating flexibility, and choose a different sprint length). The sprint ends when the selected time frame (e.g., two weeks) concludes. The next sprint begins as soon as the prior one ends.

During each sprint, the team completes the work they've committed to, facilitated using key activities: sprint planning, sprint review, and retrospective reviews.

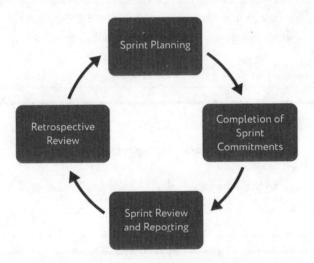

Figure 5.4: The Sprint Cycle

During sprint planning, the team identifies what they can realistically accomplish during that sprint (e.g., indicating that controls X, Y, and Z can be tested and concluded upon during the sprint). Once sprint planning is complete, the team works to meet the commitments made for that sprint (e.g., test controls X, Y, and Z and draw conclusions on those controls). During the sprint review, the collective team (auditors and the client, as well as the leaders of both the auditors and the client) inspects the results of the sprint. In the case of an audit, the team inspects the results of the audit, including any audit observations identified.

When leveraging sprint-based audit delivery, you may choose to deliver interim reports or your standard audit reports at the end of each sprint. Regardless of the report format used, the team reviews the results of the sprint during the sprint review meeting. For a two-week sprint, the sprint review should take two hours or less. In practice, I've seen this take as little as fifteen minutes for a one-month audit sprint. The brief sprint review meeting in that instance was made possible through the high levels of collaboration throughout the audit, which facilitated a very easy sprint review. We had already discussed and fully vetted the content of the interim report throughout the sprint, so the sprint review was more of a confirmation of the results to be delivered to key stakeholders and a celebration of a job well done for the collective team. Once the sprint review is complete, the auditors can communicate the results as they normally would (e.g., email the final audit report for that sprint to key stakeholders).

Finally, the team conducts a retrospective review[*] at the end of each sprint to identify what went well, as well as opportunities for improvement.

When consulting with audit organizations about conducting audits in sprints, a question I commonly receive is how to handle reporting at the end of the audit. This decision is truly up to each organization and involves a number of considerations:

- Does your audit organization issue overall opinions of the area under review?
- Do your stakeholders expect a consolidated view of Internal Audit's conclusions in the area under review?
- Do you want to communicate the progress the client made as a result of receiving audit observations sooner?

Organizations that answered "yes" to any of the above questions may want to consider delivering a consolidated report at the end of the audit. This final report includes audit observations identified throughout the audit (those identified and communicated in prior sprints as well as those identified in the final sprint). Keep in mind that the results have been communicated throughout, so consolidating the results at the end of an audit delivered iteratively or in sprints *recommunicates* at the end of the audit results identified in an earlier iteration/sprint rather than holding them until the end. If the audit organization issues overall audit opinions, the consolidated report may also include an overall opinion on the area under review. As with all other activities of a sprint-based audit, it is imperative to maintain high levels of communication and collaboration between the auditors and the clients while compiling and delivering the final report.

Delivering a consolidated report at the conclusion of the final sprint may not be the most appropriate path for all audit organizations or for every situation. If it makes the most sense for the auditors and the organization's key stakeholders to

---

[*] Retrospective reviews, including how to conduct effective retrospective reviews, are covered in greater detail in Chapter 6.

forgo the consolidated view of the area under review, the auditors may choose to deliver the results of the final sprint in the same manner as in the previous sprints. The key to this is maintaining a mindset of agility and operating in a way that facilitates agility. Each situation may be unique and necessitate different approaches to communicating results at the conclusion of the final sprint.

Do Sprints Align Precisely with Portions of a Process or the Audit Scope?

Should sprints and portions of a process* have a one-to-one relationship? Not necessarily. In many instances they won't. Keep in mind that sprints are timeboxes. You may finish auditing one portion of a process before a sprint concludes. If that happens, start auditing the next in-scope process before your sprint timebox expires or consider making your timeboxes shorter. On the other hand, you may not finish all of the work related to a particular in-scope process before the sprint ends. In this case, deliver the results of what you have at the time the sprint concludes and continue working on the tasks you haven't completed during the next sprint.

The goal is to complete everything you've prioritized during each sprint. For example, if the team decides at the beginning of a sprint to complete six control tests and deliver the results of those tests during a sprint, the team should push to deliver that.

Because of the emergent nature of the work and the culture change sometimes needed to embrace these newer ways of working, it can be difficult to accurately estimate how much work the team can complete during each sprint, particularly in the earlier stages of adoption. As the team continues to work together and become more comfortable with working in this way, they should continuously improve their predictions of what they can accomplish together during each sprint, thus eventually reducing the amount of work that gets rescheduled.

When a sprint concludes (the timebox expires), when should you start the next sprint? Immediately. To maintain momentum and reduce multitasking and context switching, the next sprint begins as soon as the previous sprint ends.

Let's briefly explore the alternative: taking a break between sprints. What would you do during the break? You'd probably focus on another audit or other work during that break. If you didn't finish the work you picked up between sprints

---

* In the example from the Iterative Delivery section of this book, the audit's scope covered three key processes: acquisition, maintenance, and retirement of assets. This question is asking whether there should be a sprint for the acquisition process, a sprint for the maintenance process, and a sprint for the process around retirement of assets.

by the time the next sprint begins, you would probably have to multitask when the next sprint starts (juggling the work you picked up between sprints with the work for the sprint that just started). This leads to context switching and wasted time.

Another option is to put down the work you picked up between sprints and shift your focus to the sprint that just started. Then you have to pick up the unfinished work one to four weeks later, when this sprint concludes, and try to remember where you left off and what you still need to do to finish those tasks. Again, this is context switching, which wastes time.

Figure 5.5: Payroll Audit Broken into Sprints

The moral of the story: start the next sprint as soon as the previous sprint concludes. You'll thank me later.

CASE STUDY John Deere

In an effort to remain relevant and continue to add value, John Deere's Internal Audit department implemented a delivery model that leverages two-week sprints. This time-boxed approach keeps the team focused on what's important and what needs to get done and ensures real-time delivery of feedback. John Deere's internal audit client has responded to this audit approach with positive feedback on the shortened time frame for receiving audit results.[2]

Meeting the IIA's Standards with Sprints or Iterative Delivery

In my own experience leading audit teams through the evolution of Auditing with Agility and during speaking engagements on this topic, auditors have expressed concern about adhering to the IIA's internal auditing standards about communicating audit results when delivering in sprints or iteratively. To address this, let's revisit the applicable standards:

2400 – COMMUNICATING RESULTS

Internal auditors must communicate the results of engagements.

2410 – CRITERIA FOR COMMUNICATING

Communications must include the engagement's objectives and scope as well as applicable conclusions, recommendations, and action plans.

2410.A1 – Final communication of engagement results must, where appropriate, contain the internal auditors' opinion and/or conclusions. When issued, an opinion or conclusion must take account of the expectations of senior management, the board, and other stakeholders and must be supported by sufficient, reliable, relevant, and useful information.

Interpretation:

Opinions at the engagement level may be ratings, conclusions, or other descriptions of the results. Such an engagement may be in relation to controls around a specific process, risk, or business unit. The formulation of such opinions requires consideration of the engagement results and their significance.

2410.A2 – Internal auditors are encouraged to acknowledge satisfactory performance in engagement communications.

2410.A3 – When releasing engagement results to parties outside the organization, the communication must include limitations on distribution and use of the results. . .

2440 – DISSEMINATING RESULTS

The chief audit executive must communicate results to the appropriate parties. . .

2440.A1 – The chief audit executive is responsible for communicating the final results to parties who can ensure that the results are given due consideration.[3]

Essentially, the standards require that internal auditors communicate results of the audit to the parties deemed appropriate by the chief audit executive. These communications must include specific data points, such as the audit objectives, scope, conclusions, recommendations, overall opinions (for organizations that choose to issue overall opinions), and the client's action plans to address any audit observations.

Although Standard 2410A.1 indicates that the requirement to communicate opinions and conclusions applies to the "final communication," it does not specify that final communications must come at the end of the entire engagement. Audit organizations may decide that the results communicated at the end of a sprint or iteration are the final results of the work completed during the corresponding sprint/iteration.

Audit organizations choosing to consider communications at the end of each sprint to be the final communications should ensure each of those communications meets the requirements outlined in the standards. For example, if your organization chooses to communicate the final results at the end of each sprint, the communication should include the following elements in order to comply with the standards:

- Audit objectives
- Scope
- Conclusions
- Recommendations
- Overall opinions (as applicable)
- Action plans

These results also must be communicated to the appropriate audience, which is defined by the standards as the "parties who can ensure the results are given due consideration."[4] Doing so enables audit organizations to deliver results iteratively while complying with the IIA's Standards.

As with the other concepts described in this book, you should choose the method that works best in each situation. Some audits may work better with a traditional sprint-based approach. Others may work best with an iterative approach with delivery driven by something other than a specific timebox, and yet others may be best performed using something completely different. The key is to focus on what will deliver the most value, including being flexible with your approach to auditing, depending on each unique situation. Another key takeaway on delivering value frequently is that regardless of whether the auditors choose to deliver iteratively or in sprints, both delivery models enable clients to begin addressing gaps sooner. Both delivery models tell a different story to key stakeholders than does a waterfall delivery model.

Think about the story told to key stakeholders with each of these approaches. Under the waterfall approach, the auditors deliver a report outlining all of the gaps identified over the last few months. The unwritten narrative to the recipients of the report (process owners, their leaders, the audit committee of the board, the CEO, etc.) is as follows: "Here are the gaps in this process that the client needs to address."

Since the client received these results earlier in the audit, they've likely already begun to address them. In some cases, perhaps they've remediated the gap and the risk no longer exists in the environment. That progress can be reflected in the results delivered at the end of the final sprint.

With this approach, the underlying narrative to the report recipients now goes something like this: "Here are the gaps we identified during the audit. While there are some items that the client still needs to address, look at all the progress they've made over the past few weeks! Some of the gaps are already fixed, and others are on their way to being remediated."

Which of these narratives makes for happier clients, auditors, and stakeholders and improves the relationship between auditors and their clients? Spoiler alert: it's the second one.

Break Down the Audit Scope into Manageable Pieces

Now that the sprints and iterations are sorted out, it's time to explore another value-driven auditing concept: breaking down the audit scope into manageable pieces.* Let's call these areas of focus. Potential outcomes associated with decomposing the scope into manageable areas of focus include greater delivery of value and less time wasted (i.e., increased effectiveness and efficiency).

Most audits can be broken down into smaller units. This can be done at the control level or the subprocess level. For instance, most organizations have a payroll function. When you decompose a payroll function, you may have the following areas of focus:[†]

---

* We started to explore this a little in the previous section, when we discussed covering multiple in-scope processes in an audit, like the processes to acquire, maintain, and retire assets. Here we explore this in greater depth.

† Note: This is an illustrative example, and the specific areas of focus and prioritization will be unique for each organization.

- Setting the payroll policy
- Onboarding and offboarding associates
- Pay inputs
- Pay calculations
- Distribution of pay
- The application used to process payroll

Since the focus of this section is *value-driven* auditing, the next step for the auditors is to work with the payroll team to understand the relative priority of these areas of focus. If the auditors could only audit two or three items on the list, which should they focus on?

You likely have determined that you need to cover each of the areas of focus, but asking the question of which items are the most important to the organization reveals the areas where Internal Audit can add the most value. Using those insights, the auditors may order the list as follows, from the highest priority (e.g., the activities that absolutely *have* to be done correctly, the activities that if done incorrectly would have the greatest negative impact on the organization, the activities least understood or most recently subject to change, those that pose the greatest risk to the organization) to the lowest:

1. Onboarding and offboarding associates
2. The application used to process payroll
3. Pay calculations
4. Pay inputs
5. Distribution of pay
6. Setting the pay policy

Armed with the knowledge of which areas of focus are the highest priority, the audit team moves forward with the top one or two areas of focus. When the auditors complete the work for the first area(s) of focus, they reevaluate and reprioritize the list of remaining areas of focus with the client. They do this by asking the following questions:

- Are the items on the list still relevant?
- Are we missing anything?
- Would we add or remove anything based on what we know now?
- Has anything changed since we last reviewed this list that would change the priority of the items listed?

Once the prioritized list of focus areas is reviewed and updated as needed, the team selects the next item(s) from the list to focus on. If something falls off the list and is no longer a priority, the auditors save everyone time by not auditing that area. Key risks, controls, testing procedures, and necessary evidence are outlined in another working session that includes all auditors assigned to the audit and all of the members of the client accountable and responsible for the newly selected area(s) of focus. The cycle looks something like this:

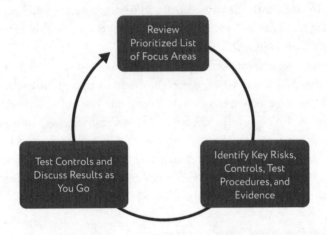

Figure 5.6: Areas of Focus Cycle

Auditors adopting a sprint-based delivery model sometimes confuse areas of focus with sprints. Remember, sprints are timeboxes, which may or may not align directly with specific areas of focus. Auditors may be able to cover one or more areas of focus in a single sprint. Or maybe not. It really depends on a number of factors, including (but not limited to) number and skill level of auditors on the engagement, number and complexity of controls within each area of focus, the length of time chosen for a sprint, etc.

The concept of dividing the audit scope into areas of focus can be paired with sprint-based delivery or a different form of iterative delivery. As alluded to earlier in this chapter, teams can choose to deliver results iteratively, once the work on a specific area of focus is complete (thus essentially reducing the length of the time-box) rather than waiting for a specific timebox (sprint) to expire or waiting until the end of the audit.

Circling back to the smorgasbord concept, delivering value frequently is like a biscuit. You can choose to have a plain biscuit (create your own way of delivering value frequently) or you can add butter (deliver value frequently through sprints) or gravy to that biscuit (deliver value frequently through iterative delivery aligned with areas of focus). I'm sure there are other ways to enjoy a biscuit, just as there are other ways to deliver value frequently. Get creative! Keep in mind what you're ultimately trying to accomplish, and let that drive your choices.

Note for clients: Here's where you can really help out on an audit and improve your own team's experience during the audit. While your auditor friends may come with a preliminary decomposition of your process or product, you and your team are well positioned to fine-tune that decomposition since you're the experts in your process or product. Recognize that your auditors can't have the same level of expertise for each area they audit. Bring your expertise to the table and help them understand how to more effectively break down your area of accountability into sections that make the most sense. You also have an important prioritization lens that the auditors need to hear. To maintain their independence and objectivity, the final list of focus areas and order of priorities may not exactly match yours (the auditors will apply their own perspective to the decomposition and prioritization, since they are experts in risk and control and bring an organization-wide perspective to their work). However, your input on these items will spread knowledge across the larger audit team, adding greater value to your specific product or process and the overall organization you both serve.

CASE STUDY Fortune 100 Insurance Company

For one audit, our team compiled a list of risks to consider for inclusion in the current audit's scope. We discussed this list of risks with key members of the client team to confirm the list was complete (were we missing anything?) and to prioritize the list by level of risk/value. To facilitate the discussion, we asked questions like:

- What are the most important or relevant risks on the list?
- If we could only cover two to three risks on this list and had to skip the rest, which should we cover?
- For which of these risks are you most heavily dependent upon effective controls to keep the risk levels manageable?
- What has to go right?

We then selected the highest priority risk as the first area of focus for the audit. Because we also chose to deliver this audit in sprints, we focused on the highest priority risk/focus area during the first sprint of the audit.

At the end of the first sprint, the team reviewed the prioritized list of risks that was developed before the start of the first sprint. We confirmed the comprehensiveness of the list (has anything changed in the last thirty days that would cause us to add or remove risks from the list?), as well as the priority of each risk on the list (has anything changed in the last thirty days that would cause a change in prioritization?). This didn't take very long, as we had grown accustomed to collaborating and working together during the first sprint.

The team finished the work planned for completion in the second sprint twenty days into the thirty-day sprint. Since there were ten days left in the sprint, the team reconvened in a working session to reevaluate the list of risks in-scope for the audit. In the working session, the team reevaluated the comprehensiveness of the list, confirmed the priority rating of each risk, and determined which items to focus on next. Everyone in the working session was highly engaged and brought diverse perspectives about the level of risk, value, and priority to the discussion. As a result, everyone agreed on what risks to focus on next, which risks needed to be included in upcoming sprints, and which were of little value or risk and could be excluded from the audit's scope.

Measure Progress through the Delivery of Value

Internal auditing, by definition, is designed to add value to an organization. Remember, the IIA defines internal auditing as "an independent, objective assurance and consulting activity designed to *add* value and improve an organization's operations [emphasis added]."[5] If Internal Audit is designed to *add value*, then delivery of that value should be the primary measure of success. The goal of an audit report is not to showcase the work performed by the auditors; rather, it is to deliver value to the organization through risk assurance and insights. Delivery of assurance and insights can include insights on how the client can increase efficiency or effectiveness of their processes, thus delivering value through achievement of outcomes.

Audit organizations often use other measures of progress, and while these can be helpful in evaluating the audit organization's effectiveness, these should not be the primary measure of progress when focusing on value-driven auditing. Here are some examples of other measures that are more output-focused rather than focused on desired outcomes:

Measuring the number of controls tested: The value of completing a control test isn't realized until auditors communicate the results of that control test to the client. Knowing the number of controls to be tested in an audit enables teams to measure progress made during the audit; however, this should not be the *primary* measure of progress, as it does not directly result in value to the key stakeholders. What happens if the auditors set out to test six controls in an audit, and after testing four of those controls, they learn that there is no value in testing the remaining two controls? This metric incentivizes the auditors to keep testing the remaining two controls, even though there is no value in doing so. Instead, what would add more value to the organization in this instance is for the auditors to *stop* and not test those two remaining controls.

Measuring the number of audit observations: Not only can this measure incentivize the wrong behavior (documenting audit observations that do not create value to the organization for the sake of having more audit observations), but it also may not provide an accurate measure of progress. Just like with control testing, the value of audit observations is not realized until auditors communicate those observations to the client. Targeting a specific number of audit observations to identify in an audit should not be a measure of progress.

If the examples provided above become the primary focus of the audit teams, teams may lose sight of their purpose of adding value. These measures also reduce client buy-in on the audit activity—they're not going to buy in to investing their time to simply so the auditors increase the number of audit observations identified (without a direct tie to value in those observations) or to have audit test more controls for the sake of testing more controls.

Even teams on a journey to better ways of working through Auditing with Agility can fall into the trap of measuring success via outputs rather than outcomes (e.g., delivery of value). I made this misstep in my own journey—and learned from it! Here's what happened:

After embarking the Agile journey in Internal Audit, I struggled with how to measure our progress. I could sense that we were progressing, but I couldn't articulate it. My peers and I started by translating the Agile Principles of Software Development into Agile Auditing principles (similar to the Principles of Auditing with Agility in this book's appendix).

We then created a scale for each principle and evaluated the current and target states for each principle. For example, for the principle of delivering value frequently, the scale to measure progress was the percentage of audits delivered in sprints.

While this seemed like the answer at first, we quickly realized it was more form over substance—more output focused than outcome focused. It didn't really show progress against our overarching goal of increasing effectiveness and efficiency of the audit process.

Like many other instances in my life, I learned a lot from this misstep. We then switched to a more outcome-focused measurement of progress: increased collaboration with clients (e.g., did our clients have the opportunity to actively participate in the development of the audit's scope?), increased timeliness of audit communications, decreased disruption to client's daily work, etc.

So, how can you measure delivery of value? Because value may be defined differently for each organization or area under review, this may look different from one organization or audit to the next.

One consistent way to measure delivery of value is to solicit feedback from key stakeholders. In my experience, the client has been more than willing to share feedback during and at the end of an audit, both positive and constructive feedback. By seeking feedback specific to value, as defined by stakeholders, auditors can better assess the extent to which they've delivered value to the organization.

As a starting point, many organizations favor effectiveness and efficiency. Determine how you can increase effectiveness or efficiency in the area under review, and you're off to a great start.

CASE STUDY Fortune 100 Insurance Company

During a retrospective review of one audit, we asked our clients how they defined value from Internal Audit. Our clients offered up the following as measurements of value:

- Focusing on areas of greatest risk or concern
- Predictability of audit work, which enabled the client to plan resources more effectively
- Finishing work in process through focused efforts before starting new work

This feedback helped me determine how successful subsequent audits were.

We continue to work with our clients on each audit to understand how best to increase the predictability of audit work for both the auditors and nonauditors. For example, we now share the risks, controls, and planned test procedures with people beyond those individuals directly involved in determining and documenting them. This helps our clients anticipate the level of effort required on their part during the audit, which lets them balance their nonaudit work and their audit work better.

Finishing work in process before starting new work is something we continue to improve. Many audit tasks have dependencies (e.g., to progress a task, clients must provide evidence, auditors must quickly obtain data from source systems, or auditors must discuss results with buy executives). While this is a work in process for us (no pun intended), we know we need to limit what's on our plates concurrently. That awareness alone has reduced the stress and confusion we often experience when juggling too many tasks at once.

Another way of measuring delivery of value is through measures associated with an intentional focus on outcomes, like time saved from one year's audit to the next, reduced lead time, progress made by the client on addressing audit observations during the audit rather than months afterward, or helping teams improve their ways of working, leading to better outcomes for the organization. Let's explore one outcome-driven measure of success: reducing lead time.

Reducing Lead Time

Lead time is the time between initiating an activity and completing that activity. For an audit, think of lead time as the time between when an audit is added to the audit plan and when the audit team communicates results to the client (delivery of value to the client).

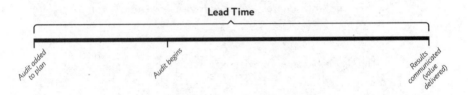

Figure 5.7: Lead Time in an Audit

Reducing lead time for audits means reducing the time between identifying the need to perform audit work in an area and communicating results of that work. This is important because including work on the audit plan means that it is important to do that work; the auditors have considered the organization's top objectives and the risks that could prevent the organization from achieving those objectives when adding that work to the plan. They've also considered the value to the organization when determining what to include in the audit plan. Therefore, they'll want to get that value into the client's hands sooner for those areas. Reducing lead time helps teams achieve that.

Teams can reduce lead time by:

1. reducing the amount of time between adding an audit to the plan and beginning the audit,
2. reducing the time between starting the audit and delivering results, or
3. both (1) and (2).

To reduce the time between adding the audit to the plan and beginning the audit, consider transitioning from an annual risk assessment and audit plan to a continuous risk assessment and a rolling audit planning process. Continuous risk assessment and a rolling audit plan are both ways to practice adaptable auditing and are covered in greater detail in Chapter 7.

Auditors can reduce the amount of time between starting an audit and communicating results by delivering audit work frequently. Saving time and facilitating the client's ability to address risk exposure sooner are both measurable examples of auditors delivering value.

Increase Visibility

Like technology work, where the concept of making work visible has gained popularity, most audit work is inherently invisible. The granular tasks that take an audit from the audit plan to the audit report (or results delivered to stakeholders) are not easily seen by those both inside and outside of the audit team. How long each task takes or how long each is delayed is often difficult to know in an audit. Making the invisible work *visible* creates transparency, enables solutions earlier, enables rapid response to change, and increases efficiency.

A common way teams increase visibility and make invisible work visible is to use a task board. Task boards can be physical (e.g., a dry-erase board with sticky-notes) or digital (e.g., a Jira* board or Microsoft Planner† board). Dry-erase boards can be effective when teams are colocated in the same physical location. In today's world of remote and hybrid work, digital task boards tend to be more effective, as they can be viewed and updated from any location. Let's walk through an example to illustrate how to make audit work visible using a task board. As we walk through this example, keep in mind that the tool is secondary to the process. It's important to figure out how you want your process to work, and then choose the tool that best supports your process.

First, set up a task board for the audit organization, a specific audit team, or an individual audit, depending on the scale at which you want to implement these practices. That scale will depend on many factors, including your organization's readiness and appetite to move to this way of working.

For example, if a single audit team wants to leverage a task board to manage their team's work, they could create a board to represent all of the team's work. The team uses initiatives, epics, and tasks. Each initiative comprises one or more epic, and each epic comprises multiple tasks.

---

* Jira is a project-management tool created by the company Atlassian.
† Planner is a task-management tool on Microsoft's 365 platform.

Initiatives are high-level categories of work that align with the team's or organization's performance objectives. Examples of initiatives include the following:

- Delivery of the audit plan
- Training and development
- Client relationship management

Epics represent large chunks of work (in support of the initiatives) to be broken down into smaller tasks. Examples of epics may include the following:

- Audit engagements
- Audit observation follow-up
- Risk assessment activities
- Development planning
- Job shadowing
- Training

Tasks are individual activities to complete in support of each epic. Examples of tasks include, but are certainly not limited to, the following:

- Document planning meeting #1
- Document planning meeting #2
- Risk and control matrix
- Process flows
- Opening meeting
- Workpaper #1
- Workpaper #2
- Workpaper #3
- Closing/exit meeting
- Communication of audit results

Each task should contain, at a minimum, a title, description of what it takes for the task to be considered "done," and an estimate of the effort required to complete the task[*] (i.e., to take a task from "to do" to "done").[†]

---

[*] Sometimes called story points in the Scrum framework. The appendix contains more information on story points.

[†] There are a variety of ways to estimate effort and assign points. Check out the appendices for more information on estimating story points.

The task board should include columns representing the stages through which each task must flow prior to completion. If most audit tasks require work to be done, reviewed by a peer or an auditor in charge (AIC), and finally reviewed by the audit lead, then the columns on the board may include To Do, In Process, Peer Review, Lead Review, and Done.

Next, the team should break down tasks at a level granular enough to be completed within a reasonable amount of time without having to pick the task up, put it down (e.g., to wait for a dependency to be cleared), pick it back up again, and so forth. Each time the task is put down before it is complete, inefficiencies are introduced due to context switching.

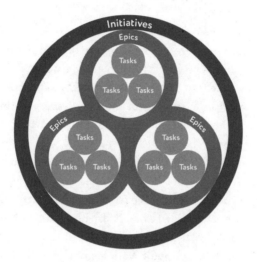

Figure 5.8: Initiatives, Epics, Tasks

Each task is assigned to one person. The assignee on a task is responsible for completing the task and getting it through required reviews or steps through completion. It may be intuitive to reassign the task to the reviewer when the task is ready for review, but this leads to inefficiencies because the reviewer then needs to remember who was ultimately responsible for completing the card and reassign it to that person if they need to address review comments. Instead, reviewers should monitor the "Peer Review" and "Lead Review" columns on the board. When cards are moved into those columns, reviewers know that those tasks are ready to be reviewed, and by whom. They also know who to provide review comments to: the assignee on the card. Alternatively, task assignees could tag reviewers on the digital task board.

It is important to clearly define what "done" looks like for each task and to notate this on each card. For example, there may be a card representing a test of a control's design. Several things must happen for that card to be completed (i.e., before it can be moved to the "Done" column):

1. The workpaper must be created in the tool used to document audit work.
2. The test of design must be completed and documented in the workpaper.
3. A conclusion must be reached and vetted with the client.
4. The workpaper must be reviewed by the auditor in charge.
5. Review comments must be addressed.
6. The workpaper must be approved in the audit tool by the auditor in charge.

Each task will have its own unique definition of done, and each organization or team may use a different level of granularity to break down tasks.

The task board should be visible to all involved parties. To maintain independence, auditors may choose to limit the client's access to the board to be read-only or to limit access only to the audit team and their leaders. If this is the case, the auditors need to communicate frequently with the client to make sure the client maintains awareness of the board.

Making work visible to audit leaders helps them identify and address capacity constraints or unnecessary work (i.e., work that does not support achievement of the team's global goals), enabling the team to shift away from the unnecessary work and toward more value-added work. It also helps the audit staff better understand how their work supports global goals.

Increasing the visibility of audit work also helps identify and resolve bottlenecks. For example, if cards pile up in the "Peer Review" queue, the team can identify another associate with the appropriate authority to step in and help review, thus relieving the bottleneck and getting the value (conclusions) into the client's hands sooner. This also makes the prioritization of tasks transparent, so the team knows which tasks to tackle first. As a bonus, some task board tools like Jira and Microsoft Planner make prioritization visible through a capability to assign priority levels to tasks.

Auditors should add all work to the board, even tasks that are not directly tied to a specific audit. All work should align to the audit organization's objectives. That is, the tasks should align with one of the initiatives on the team's task board. This is all about staying focused on value delivery.

As a reminder, initiatives represent the audit organization's goals or strategic priorities. Adding work to the team's task board links the work to overarching objectives. If a task can't easily be linked or aligned to an objective or initiative, the team should challenge whether that particular task is necessary. Below are examples of work to include on the task board:

- Periodic meetings with the client outside of an audit as part of ongoing risk assessment activities
  - This supports the audit team's objective to evaluate the effectiveness of risk management processes to help the organization achieve its objectives.
  - This also supports adherence with the IIA's Performance Standard 2010, which requires auditors to consult with senior management to understand the organization's strategies, objectives, and risks.
- Training
  - Training supports the audit organization's objectives through adherence with the IIA's Attribute Standard 1210, which requires internal auditors to possess the knowledge, skills, and competencies needed to perform their responsibilities.
  - Training also supports adherence with the IIA's Attribute Standard 1230, which requires internal auditors to enhance knowledge, skills, and competencies through continuing professional development.
- Meeting with pipeline talent or reviewing resumes
  - This activity supports adherence with the IIA's Performance Standard 2030, which requires chief audit executives to ensure that audit resources are "appropriate, sufficient, and effectively deployed to achieve the approved plan."[6]
  - This also supports the audit organization's ability to add value and improve the organization's operations.
- Preparing audit committee materials
  - This directly supports adherence with the IIA's Performance Standard 2060 – Reporting to Senior Management and the Board.

In addition to making invisible audit work visible, these practices help create more transparency, which drives additional value to the organization.

When using a traditional audit approach, the auditor in charge meets with the audit team periodically (typically weekly) to get an updated status of the audit. The audit staff often provides a verbal update to the AIC on where they are with their work. If anyone assigned to the audit is out of the office during the weekly status update, either the AIC reaches out to the team member who was out of the office separately to get their status, or the AIC waits until the next week to get an update. The AIC has to keep their leader informed of the audit's status and any roadblocks as well. If the audit leader has questions, the AIC has to go back to the staff to get an answer. Playing a game of telephone was fun in elementary school, but who has the time or patience for that at work?

By increasing visibility into audit work, auditors can save the games for the weekends or for after-work happy hours.

When work is made visible by using a physical or virtual task board, the entire team has instant access to the status of the audit work without having to ask anyone or set up a meeting. Yes, you read that correctly: you don't have to have a meeting to provide your leader with an update of where everything stands with the audit work! Even better, your board will illuminate which items have impediments blocking them. Team members with authority will instantly know what's needed to unblock those items. Again, there's no need to schedule a separate meeting to accomplish this. All anyone has to do is walk over to the physical task board or pull up the digital task board on their computer.

For teams that aren't yet ready to make the leap into managing work using task boards, there are other ways to increase visibility without wholeheartedly changing the way of working. Using shared documents or posting questions in a shared chat are great examples. Shared documents within collaboration tools, like Microsoft Teams or Google Docs, enable more than one user to make edits while providing version control. Sending a question to a group chat (that includes both auditors and the client) creates visibility for all involved parties. This reduces duplicate requests to clients and decreases the likelihood that auditors will get bounced around to a number of different client contacts to get the requested information. Organizations can use this as a stepping stone to increase visibility immediately. I encourage teams not to stop there, though. If leveraging shared documents is your first step to increasing visibility, go ahead and implement that today, with an eye on what you can implement tomorrow to further increase visibility and start achieving your desired outcomes. The key here is to focus on desired outcomes and proceed with an open mind and an attitude of innovation, continuous experimentation and learning.

> **Note for clients:** If your team uses the concepts described in this
> section, look for ways to incorporate the work associated with
> an audit into your own ways of increasing visibility. Do you use
> Jira to manage workflow and create visibility into the status of

specific tasks? Great! Perhaps you can have the audit team create Jira cards for audit-related tasks your team is expected to complete. Would it also be helpful to have visibility into the tasks the audit team is working on? If yes, consider a shared task board where tasks for all parties involved in the audit are visible. If your auditors don't already use task boards to create visibility, it may be a worthwhile investment to teach them. It may end up being a skill set and a practice they can incorporate on other audits to improve their own ways of working. If they only use it on the audit of the process that falls within your team's scope of accountability, that's okay too. You can both experience the benefits of working in this way; for your team, that's primarily a reduction in the unexpected disruption for your team that often occurs when an audit begins.

Constantly Optimize for the Global Goals Rather than Individual Goals

Global goals for auditors are the same as the audit organization's goals. Per the auditing profession's definition, the goals of internal audit are to:

- Add value and improve the organization's operations
- Help the organization accomplish its objectives (note that this is also a global goal shared with the client)
- Evaluate and improve the effectiveness of risk management, control, and governance processes

Internal Audit organizations may also have additional goals supplementing these profession-wide goals, such as:

- Incorporating agility into the audit process
- Leveraging data and analytics to provide greater assurance or more valuable insights to the client
- Automating manual processes to increase efficiency

Individual goals are unique to each person. These individual goals may indeed support one or more global goals; however, at times they may not. For example, learning how to perform Auditing with Agility supports all of the global audit goals, specifically the global goal of adding value to an organization's operations. It also supports the audit organization's goal of incorporating agility into the audit process. Conversely, an individual goal of learning how to code in Visual Basic (VBA), when VBA is not endorsed or used by the organization, may not directly support achievement of a global goal. Let's explore another example to further illustrate.

A global goal for a specific audit may be to evaluate controls in the payroll process. Work performed digging into incentive programs may not support the audit's goal (particularly if incentive programs are covered in a separate audit). If the audit team begins to dig into the incentive programs, they should challenge each other and evaluate whether that work directly supports the audit's global goal of evaluating controls in the payroll process. If they determine that that work does not support the global goal, the team should table the incentive program work until it can be aligned with a global goal and do the incentive program work in alignment with the appropriate global goal.[*] This helps minimize the risk of scope creep during an audit. It also enables the team to stop auditing when they determine the residual value of continuing with the audit is minimal.

> **CASE STUDY** Fortune 100 Insurance Company
>
> Recall the experiences we explored in Chapter 2. My team and I optimized for the global goal (focusing on what's best for the organization) rather than individual goals (the client's goals versus the auditors' goals) by rebranding ourselves as THE team. We were no longer the auditors and the client with separate goals. We were one team committed to a global goal: delivering value through providing assurance on key controls within the process under review. This created greater buy-in from our clients, as they understood and believed in the goal we collectively sought to achieve. It strengthened our working relationships as well because we worked together, not against each other. This example has elements of both value-driven auditing and integrated auditing. Let's transition into integrated auditing concepts next.

---

[*] Or, if the incentive program has risen in priority, the team can pivot to auditing that area in support of the global goal of auditing the most important areas of the organization.

Chapter 6

Practices and Principles of Integrated Auditing 2.0

As I mentioned earlier, Integrated Auditing 1.0 is a practice that integrated technology, financial, and operational auditing into a single audit. Before Integrated Auditing 1.0, these types of audits were performed separately and either reported separately or pieced together at the end of the audit. Integrated Auditing 2.0 takes this concept a step further by integrating audit work into the client's daily work and integrating continuous improvement into the audit process.

Integrating audit work into the client's work creates less interruption to the client's daily work (keeping them primarily focused on working toward the organization's objectives), facilitates a stronger collective knowledge and perspective of the area being audited, resolves roadblocks sooner, and more clearly aligns auditors and their clients on a collective goal rather than pitting them against each other.

In this chapter, we'll go over several strategies that can help integrate auditing practices into the client's work:

- Practice intentional collaboration.
- Work together daily.
- Work as a single team toward a collective goal.
- Use integrated planning.
- Create feedback loops.

Intentional Collaboration

Audits conducted using the traditional waterfall approach depend, to a certain extent, on collaboration with the client. Even audits performed using an older way of working cannot be completed without some level of interaction with the client. Auditing with Agility takes a more intentional approach to collaboration and integrates that collaboration into the team's daily work.

Under the traditional audit approach, the auditor in charge interviews the process owner (or the product owner when auditing a specific technology or product) to understand the process (or product) under review, uses that information to identify key risks and controls to audit, and presents that information to the audit team and the client. These groups then negotiate on what is in scope and document the rationale for including these items in the audit's scope, or for excluding certain items from the scope.

With Auditing with Agility, the entire audit team (not just the auditor in charge, as is common during waterfall audits) works with the client to understand the in-scope process or product; identify key risks, controls, and testing procedures; and define scope boundaries. To preserve objectivity and independence, the auditors retain ultimate decision rights.

Collaborating with the client through the entire audit planning process creates buy-in from the beginning—from both the client and the audit team—and reduces negotiations. It also helps the client feel like they are part of the audit (because they are!)—like they are participating in the audit rather than being subjected to an audit.

Similarly, when the auditor in charge gives the audit staff a say in planning the audit rather than telling them the scope and sending them on their way into fieldwork, they too feel included in the audit and contribute to building the audit's scope. This not only creates buy-in from both audit staff and the client but also leverages diverse perspectives to define the scope and promotes effective challenge of the audit scope. This reduces negotiations on the audit scope from both the client and from within the audit team, replacing those negotiations with collaboration.

Negotiations also occur when discussing audit results, particularly when audit observations are identified. Strong collaboration between auditors and the client leads to staff members identifying audit observations earlier in the process. For instance, when planning an audit together, the collective team (auditors and the client) may identify gaps together before any testing even begins. At this early stage, everyone has aligned on the applicable risks, and when identifying controls in place to mitigate those risks, oftentimes these collaborative discussions encourage the client to identify gaps themselves. It goes something like this:

Auditor: Thank you for walking us through your team's objectives and helping us understand what goals are most important to your team. Let's think about what could get in the way of achieving those objectives. It seems like promoting bad code to production could be a relevant risk.

Client: Close, but really, the true risk is that we promote code that doesn't do what we expect it to do or that breaks things when we move it to production.

Auditor: That makes much more sense. So, what do you do to ensure code that doesn't do what you expect or that breaks things isn't promoted to production?

Client: We require peer reviews of all code prior to moving it to production.

Auditor: Excellent! How do you enforce that requirement? Said another way, what prevents someone from skipping the peer review step or detects when the peer review was skipped?

Client: Hmm. We know peer reviews are important, but there isn't anything that would prevent someone from skipping that step. That seems like a problem, because if someone skipped the peer review, the code might not work or it could break things in production.

Auditor: It sounds like there's a control gap that we should document as an audit observation, would you agree?

Client: Absolutely. The gap is that there isn't a control to make sure peer reviews occur prior to moving code into production. Without this control, we might break things or release a feature that doesn't meet our customers' needs!

Not only did the team collectively identify the gap before samples were selected, evidence requested, and testing performed, but they also agreed early in the process that there was a gap in the control environment.

As if it wasn't great enough to save everyone's time by identifying an existing gap without doing extensive testing, the client actually articulated the gap and the risk rather than the auditor. When the auditors and the client collectively presented this observation to their respective leaders, there was way more buy-in on both sides. In this case, the team chose to collaborate rather than negotiate and enjoyed greater buy-in and fewer ongoing negotiations.

This also could have been an opportunity to leverage data analytics, AI, or ML to test the population, but the client identified the gap very early on in the audit, so there was no need to spend time building those tools at this time. There certainly may be a great use case for leveraging these tools going forward in this example. Regardless, intentional collaboration between auditors and clients enabled delivery of value to key stakeholders sooner than if the teams had operated in silos.

This value also applies to internal interactions within the audit team. Collaboration tools can increase this capability. Teams can use ongoing group chats to facilitate knowledge-sharing and timely responses to inquiries and requests. These tools also enable collaboration within documents, allowing multiple team members to edit the same document simultaneously, all while providing version control.

CASE STUDY Anywhere Real Estate Inc.

After their recent audit, Anywhere Real Estate's Internal Audit team received positive feedback from their client about the increased transparency that stemmed from the team's focus on high levels of collaboration with the client. The client strongly appreciated the collaborative approach Internal Audit took when developing the audit's scope. The audit team did this together with the client, first presenting the preliminary scope, and then providing the opportunity for the client to collaborate to solidify the scope, accounting for the client's priorities and what keeps them up at night.[1]

Auditors and Their Clients Work Together Daily

One way of creating an environment that fosters collaboration is for auditors and their clients to work together *daily*. By collaborating daily, all parties are more informed and have a voice in the audit work. This creates more buy-in and engages everyone involved. If the team identifies the need to modify the audit's scope during the audit, discussing this as soon as the need to change is identified enables decision-makers (auditors) to make well-informed decisions, and also enables affected parties (the client) to assess and respond to the impact of the change on their own daily work.

Working together daily also keeps things moving and supports an increased velocity with which work is completed and value is delivered. It also further integrates auditors into the client's daily work, which is key to adopting Auditing with Agility. Working together daily and incorporating the client's input into audit work while still maintaining final decision rights and independence shifts the client's role from *being audited* or having the audit happen to them to that of *actively participating* in the audit as part of the team. Although most of my career has been as an auditor, during my time as an audit client, I would have preferred actively participating in the audit rather than passively having the audit happen to me.

Daily collaboration can be achieved through a number of methods; one of which is by conducting daily stand-up meetings, which we'll discuss in a bit.* Other ways to facilitate working together daily include ongoing group chats using collaboration tools like Slack† or Microsoft Teams and sharing real-time status through task boards. What works for one audit organization or on one audit may not work as well for others. Organizations should maintain an agile mindset and modify the collaboration approach to best fit the needs of each situation.

> **CASE STUDY** Fortune 100 Insurance Company
>
> In one of my team's early Auditing with Agility experiments, the audit team worked together with the client frequently throughout the audit, through iterative meetings with both internal and external stakeholders. We provided weekly updates to internal stakeholders (the control owners/the client) on the status of the work and any potential audit observations identified. The audit team met with external stakeholders (the external auditors) twice each week, sent out detailed meeting notes to reiterate key decisions reached, and sought feedback and confirmation from those stakeholders after each meeting. This kept us all aligned on expectations, progress made, and next steps.

---

* Daily meetings are commonly referred to as "stand-ups." Teams hold stand-ups to share what was accomplished since the prior stand-up, what will be accomplished between now and the next stand-up, and any impediments that need to be addressed. They are called stand-ups because they should be kept short, typically fifteen minutes in length. The idea is that the stand-ups are so brief that you can conduct them standing up, as many organizations do. Conducting the meeting while standing up helps keep the meeting brief and focused.

† Slack is a business messaging application.

We quickly learned the value of auditors and the client working together frequently. In a subsequent audit, we met with our clients twice weekly to compare the experience of meeting weekly. At one point, our clients asked if we could change the frequency of our meetings. Instead of meeting twice weekly, they wanted to meet daily. It was in this audit that my team and I learned the value of working with our clients daily. Our questions and requests were addressed sooner, we were more efficient with our clients' time, and we built more rapport and had more fun through these daily interactions.

Integrating Audit into the Client's Daily Work: Working as One Team toward a Collective Goal

We previously established that Auditing with Agility has roots in Agile, specifically the Agile principles of software development and the Agile values. Auditing with Agility takes these roots and adds in the Three Ways of DevOps.

DevOps uses flow/systems thinking to emphasize the performance of the entire system, as opposed to the performance of a specific silo of work or department. *The DevOps Handbook* further explains that flow/systems thinking "accelerate[s] the delivery of work . . . to customers."[2]

Incorporating this into the audit process is a great way to experience the benefits of Integrated Auditing 2.0 and is one of the key differentiators between Auditing with Agility and Agile Auditing. By integrating audit work into the client's daily work, teams shift their focus from individual team goals to a collective goal.

In an audit that does not incorporate this type of integration, auditors and the client focus on accomplishing their own goals in silos. This can pit the two teams against each other. The audit team focuses on testing controls and delivering an audit report, and the client works to achieve their team's objectives. These two goals are distinct yet related. Both are anchored to the organization achieving its objectives, but the two siloed teams are missing out on opportunities to collaborate closely and work together to achieve those goals. Instead, an audit should be a collective commitment between auditors and the client to determine whether controls are effective to support achievement of the organization's objectives.

This alignment of performance does not change *what* the client or the auditors do. Auditors still evaluate the effectiveness of controls, and the client still performs controls. This alignment changes how both groups go about their work. By working together to accomplish the collective goal and integrating both groups' work together, the collective team becomes better positioned to accomplish the goal effectively and efficiently.

Stand-Ups

You can achieve deeper integration between auditors and the client through a number of activities, the first of which is through daily stand-ups. (We discuss stand-ups more in Chapter 7.) If the client holds daily stand-ups, ask to join them. When you've truly integrated the audit work into the client's workflow, the client will begin discussing and addressing audit tasks during their stand-ups. Integrating further by including auditors in those stand-ups creates more efficiencies by eliminating the game of telephone often played between auditors and the client. Integrating auditors into the client's stand-ups brings everyone together to address impediments.

For example, consider the situation where the client conducts daily stand-ups as part of their normal course of business. During one of these stand-ups, a client team member discusses an audit task and expresses a need for clarity from the auditors. If auditors are not included in the stand-up, the client team member must connect separately with the auditors to seek clarification. If, instead, the auditors attend the stand-up, the team member can get immediate clarity and move forward.

What if the client does not use stand-ups? While daily stand-ups are more commonly used in technology organizations or departments, auditors who add value to other parts of an organization (non-technology-focused departments) don't have to miss out on this opportunity to increase integration between auditors and the client. Instead of auditors joining the client's stand-ups, reverse the situation. Auditors host the stand-ups and include the client in them. Here, the stand-ups focus primarily on the audit, and everyone involved in the audit is present to help facilitate continued progress and removal of impediments.

Join Existing Meetings

Another way to integrate audit work with the client's work is to leverage some of the client's existing meetings, beyond daily stand-ups. For example, instead of holding a meeting solely focused on helping the auditors understand how a control operates, the auditors can sit (virtually or in-person) with someone from the project team as they perform the control.

Consider a meeting between audit clients and an investment fund manager used by the client to discuss controls performed by that fund manager. An example of such a control is the audit client's ongoing due diligence to ensure the fund manager continues to have adequate controls in place. This could include the audit client periodically interviewing the fund manager or conducting on-site visits to stay informed of the fund's strategy, investments, and exposure.

In many cases, auditors request evidence that the meeting occurred, such as notes from the meeting and calendar invitations, or other due diligence documentation. This requires the audit client to dig through dusty files or hope that they saved the email with meeting notes (and that the organization's retention policy didn't delete the email). The auditors then review this documentation to determine whether it provides enough assurance that the control was performed effectively.

With the mindset of Integrated Auditing 2.0, the auditors could instead sit in on some of the audit client's meetings with the fund managers to observe the control performance (again, virtually or in person). This also facilitates real-time feedback. By testing the control performance as it's happening, the auditors can give feedback to their clients *immediately*. This enables the client to pivot if needed to increase effectiveness rather than having a long gap between when the meeting was conducted and the old dusty files were reviewed.

Pre-Implementation Reviews

Integration can also be achieved during a pre-implementation review of a new tool, environment, or process. In this type of audit, the auditors provide consulting services to their clients, helping them determine whether risks will be addressed in the new tool, environment, or process.

In many cases, the implementation team meets frequently to discuss the project and address problems. Instead of scheduling separate meetings for the audit, auditors integrate themselves into the project by joining the project implementation meetings to observe the discussions, learn about the planned control environment, and ask questions to assess the planned control environment in real time. By doing this, auditors reduce the number of unnecessary meetings, which makes everyone happier and strengthens the relationship between auditors and audit clients.

Taking this a step further, auditors can ingrain or embed themselves throughout a project (such as a business transformation, technology implementation, or a conversion). Through each stage of the project life cycle, the auditors stay connected with the client and provide assurance over the design of the controls, advice on planned controls, or recommendations on improvements and opportunities to increase effectiveness or efficiency during the project.

Integrating auditors into the early phases of the implementation or project rather than bringing them in at the end or after the tool, environment, or process has been implemented, lets the implementation team pivot as needed to strengthen the control environment while they are still able—during development rather than waiting until after implementation, when it's more costly to make changes. Collaborating with auditors early in a project's life cycle also yields many of the benefits discussed throughout this book, including stronger relationships, delivery of greater value sooner, and better positioning the organization to achieve its objectives.

The following are a few examples of what pre-implementation involvement by the audit team can provide the client:

- An independent lens on the alignment between the project's work and the business value or business case
- Determination on whether decision rights and decision-making criteria are well defined
- An evaluation of whether decisions are being made in alignment with those criteria and decision rights
- Advice on the level of testing or documentation needed to satisfy external auditors or regulatory bodies when data is being converted or transferred to a new system

Integrated Planning

In a traditional auditing approach, auditors involve the client in the planning phase incrementally. That is, the audit team meets with the client to gain a high-level understanding of the area under review, including a walkthrough of the key processes. With this understanding, the audit team identifies key controls and develops test procedures for each of the key controls in scope. The auditors compile a list of documentation needed to perform the tests and provide that request list to the client, who then takes the request list and pulls together documentation for the auditors. While this requires some collaboration between auditors and the client, the auditors play an active role and the client plays more of a passive role. Auditing with Agility takes integration during planning a step further.

Integrated planning includes the entire audit team assigned to the audit, as well as the client, in the identification of key risks, key controls, testing procedures, and request list creation. Who knows the area under review better than the clients who work in that space every day? You got it . . . no one knows it better than the client.

By using integrated planning, where both the client and auditors actively develop the scope, test procedures, and request list, the resulting audit program (which outlines the procedures the auditors will follow to complete the audit) is better understood by all parties. The auditors better understand what risks and controls are most relevant to the area under review, and the client understands how the auditors intend to test those controls. The audit is focused on delivering value in the most relevant areas. What's even better is that the client knows exactly what documentation to provide to the auditors, and the auditors know exactly what to expect from the client and how to use it for their tests.

If, on your trip through the value-driven auditing section of the Auditing with Agility smorgasbord, you decided to divide your scope into prioritized areas of focus, you can tackle planning for each area of focus in either a single meeting or multiple meetings held on the same day. I've been in a planning meeting where the group met for an hour, took a break, and reconvened for another hour. This approach was helpful because the break gave the team time to digest information from the first hour and identify any questions or clarification we needed to obtain during the second session. If you choose to break the planning into more than one meeting, be sure to keep those meetings close together, preferably on the same day. Otherwise, you may end up multitasking between meetings (rather than taking time to digest and prepare for the next session) and doing a lot of context switching. This can reduce your effectiveness in planning and create inefficiencies.

How might this play out in practice? Let's revisit the payroll example, where the auditors are conducting an audit of the organization's payroll process. The auditors decomposed the payroll process into prioritized areas of focus, leveraging the payroll team's input and expertise, and selected the areas of focus with highest priority to tackle first. The auditors now continue working with the payroll team to understand the key risks associated with the selected areas of focus and to identify the key controls the client performs to manage those risks. This is accomplished through one or more meetings that include the auditors assigned to the audit and the client responsible for the selected areas of focus. During the meeting(s), the group also collaboratively identifies the most effective way to test the controls and requests supporting evidence. Rather than the auditors determining how to test the controls and what evidence is needed without the help of the individuals who perform the controls, with this approach, the client is part of the discussion, which creates efficiencies by reducing confusion or opportunities for miscommunication.

As an auditor, how many times have you requested documentation from the client and received something totally different from what you expected? As someone who has been audited, how many times have you provided what was asked of you, just to find out the auditors needed something different? For both the auditors and the clients, this is frustrating. I asked a similar question to an audience of about a thousand technology leaders while presenting at the 2022 DevOps Enterprise Summit. Most, if not all, of the audience raised their hands, indicating that they've also experienced this situation. By covering the necessary evidence in the same discussion where the team collectively identifies risks and controls, there is greater alignment between both auditors and the client on not only the scope, but also the documentation needed to test the in-scope controls. This reduces the chances of misunderstandings about the scope, testing approach, and evidence the client needs to provide to the auditors.

Let's get back to the payroll audit example. Because all of the auditors assigned to the audit actively participated in the initial meeting to identify risks, controls, and evidence, there is no need to hold a separate meeting between the auditor in charge and the audit staff to bring everyone up to speed. The staff were also empowered during that initial meeting to ask clarifying questions, so they all clearly understood each of the controls and are now well positioned to take on any of the in-scope control tests. They're able to connect the dots from one control to the next to understand dependencies and compensating controls. The information gathered in the initial audit meeting is typically sufficient to document and evaluate the design of the controls as well. While the auditors document the design of the controls within the first area(s) of focus, the client starts sending over the agreed-upon documentation. Because the client was included in the initial audit discussion and they know what documentation to provide the auditors, the audit requests typically get fulfilled much sooner and the auditors can begin testing operating effectiveness earlier than when using the traditional approach.

CASE STUDY Fortune 100 Insurance Company

When we experimented with integrated planning, we (auditors and the client) discussed what risk to focus on first and decided to focus on the highest priority risk. Our next step was to determine the key controls in place to mitigate that risk. In a traditional audit approach, we would conduct a number of planning meetings with the client over the course of a few weeks to identify the key controls. This didn't fit into the approach we took for this audit, so the collective team swarmed around the task at hand: identifying key controls for the highest priority risk. By including all key members of the team, we created efficiencies and increased knowledge sharing. Instead of starting a meeting talking about control A, realizing the person we were meeting with was really responsible for control B, and having to schedule a separate meeting with a different person to discuss control A, all the key contacts were included in this meeting. The client representatives on the team who were responsible for all key controls related to the risk we covered in this portion of the audit were in attendance, so we were able to identify all of the relevant controls in one meeting. To keep us on track and enable us to accomplish this, the team clearly defined objectives for this meeting, including

- identifying key controls to test,
- determining appropriate test procedures,
- identifying and requesting data or documentation needed to complete testing, and
- agreeing about what needed to occur within the next thirty days.

For the last item on the list above, the team committed to fulfilling audit requests, conducting control walkthroughs, completing control tests, working through testing results together, and delivering an interim audit report for the work completed. This approach set clear expectations for everyone involved and set us up for success for the next thirty days and throughout the rest of the audit. We were collectively aligned on the scope and approach, and we all bought into our commitments.

Feedback Loops

Feedback loops are another element of integrated auditing that evolved from both Agile and DevOps. Using this element of integrated auditing, teams intentionally seek feedback on how to increase effectiveness and modify behaviors to incorporate that feedback. Auditing with Agility encourages auditors to pause periodically throughout each audit to solicit feedback from involved parties, including auditors, the client, and other key stakeholders.

It's difficult, if not impossible, to address or fix what you aren't aware of. Additionally, simply *becoming aware* of an opportunity to become more effective without *acting* to become more effective is pretty useless. You're reading this book and, in doing so, will identify ways to increase your team's effectiveness. If you do nothing with that knowledge, you won't experience any of the benefits of better ways of working. You must adjust your (and your team's) behavior to increase efficiency and effectiveness.

In the integrated planning section, we explored how systems/flow thinking can help achieve the benefits of integrated auditing by facilitating a left-to-right flow of information:

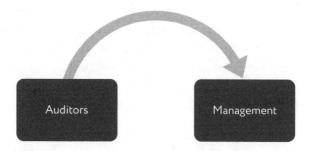

**Figure 6.1: Integrating Audit into the Client's Daily Work
(Systems/Flow Thinking)**

Well, feedback loops are simply the converse of systems/flow thinking, a right-to-left flow:

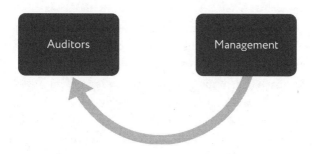

Figure 6.2: Feedback Loops

The objective of feedback loops is to make "work safer by creating fast, frequent, high quality information flow."[3] This enables teams to address problems before they compile into larger problems. It also enables team learning to prevent the same problems from reoccurring.

Feedback loops are an important concept for Auditing with Agility. Using feedback loops, teams intentionally solicit feedback from relevant and impacted parties, including auditors and key members of the client involved in the audit. Intentionally soliciting feedback and taking action on that feedback lets everyone feel heard, which increases everyone's level of engagement and strengthens the relationship between auditors and audit clients. There are a number of ways to incorporate feedback loops during an audit, including retrospective reviews and real-time feedback.

Retrospective Reviews

Recall that retrospective reviews are discussions to reflect and identify, as a team, what went well and what should be improved going forward. The retrospective review's objective is to improve during the next audit, sprint, iteration, etc.

Retrospective reviews are one of the simplest yet most effective practices to help you delight your stakeholders using Auditing with Agility. The frequency and timing of these reviews will vary depending on the approach used on a particular audit.

Auditors continuing to leverage the traditional waterfall approach may perform a retrospective review at the end of the audit, facilitating changes in behavior that will benefit the next client team under review. This might happen through either digital surveys or facilitated discussions. Soliciting feedback from the client at the end of the audit enables a full-picture view of the audit experience and provides the auditors with information on what went well and should continue in future audits, as well as what can be improved upon in the next audit.

While retrospective reviews are useful tools, they have limitations when not paired with other sources of feedback. One such limitation is that the individuals who provide feedback at the end of the audit may not experience the benefits of providing feedback (e.g., improved audit processes and improved audit experiences). In many cases, the auditors will not return to audit the same clients and areas for a year or longer. Another limitation is that soliciting feedback only at the end of the audit doesn't give the team a chance to improve the audit work or the client's experience *during* the audit. After all, you can't fix what you aren't aware of. Another limitation of waiting until the end of the audit to solicit feedback is the recency bias. When the client provides feedback only at the end of the audit, there's a strong likelihood that the feedback will be heavily weighted to the events that happened most recently. Auditors may miss out on feedback that could help them provide a better experience for the client on earlier parts of the audit due to this bias.

Auditors leveraging the Agile Auditing framework or an approach that delivers results in iterations will perform retrospective reviews at the end of each sprint or iteration to change behavior during the next sprint. This enables the team to experience the benefits of addressing feedback during the audit rather than waiting until the end of the audit. It can also reduce the effects of recency bias.

Audits performed with a more loosely defined delivery model (e.g., delivery not tied to specific time-based triggers like the end of the audit or the end of a sprint) intentionally pause throughout the audit (at whatever points in time that seem most appropriate to solicit feedback and modify behavior accordingly) to obtain feedback. Keeping in the stream of agility, teams should select the frequency and timing that best fits each unique situation.

Simply setting aside time for a retrospective review isn't enough. It is imperative to facilitate *effective* retrospective reviews, regardless of when or how frequently they are performed (at the end of the audit, regularly throughout, or on an ad-hoc basis throughout). A key driver of effectiveness with this is that these reviews must be *blameless*. It's easy to start pointing fingers and placing blame on individuals when discussing what didn't go so well. What does that accomplish? Increased defensiveness, shutting down, and arguing to win or prove a point. None of those behaviors typically result in actionable solutions or immediately improved performance.

Effective retrospective review facilitators ask intentional questions to facilitate an effective discussion, including:

- What went well?
- What can be improved in the next audit/sprint/etc.?
- What can we do differently to drive more value going forward?

Keeping the discussion focused on what to modify going forward based on what we learned in the past rather than recounting each detail of who did what and why it didn't work out keeps the conversation solution focused, not blame ridden. This is not a space to point fingers and assign blame. All that does is create defensiveness and put up walls, impeding improvement. The key is to keep retrospective reviews blameless.

Let's imagine that a group of auditors doesn't do integrated planning for an audit; instead, they develop their request list on their own. Unfortunately, it takes a couple weeks of back and forth between the auditors and the clients to finally get the right documentation to move forward with control tests. After the audit, during the retrospective review, the auditors and clients acknowledge that the audit evidence request process needs to be improved. If the auditors bring it up by saying, "The clients need to fulfill our requests sooner and more accurately," they've immediately put their clients on the defensive. The clients will fire back with "Well, your request list wasn't clear at all. I provided you what you asked for, then you asked for something else!" Instead of working together to find a solution to improve the process, everyone is in the middle of a combative argument.

Rather, they should approach it without placing blame. This time, the auditors bring it up saying, "The audit evidence request process seemed to take too long. How can we improve that?" Then nobody is on the defensive and everyone is brainstorming how to have a better experience next time around. Keep the blame out of your retrospectives and you'll keep the team focused on finding a solution rather than a scapegoat.

Further supporting the collaborative and integrated nature of Auditing with Agility, retrospective reviews should include all relevant individuals, both auditors and the client. Each individual gained a unique perspective during the audit (or sprint, or leading up to whatever triggered the retrospective review) and therefore brings diverse insights to the session.

The team may identify a large number of improvement opportunities during a retrospective review. That's great! Keep the brainstorming session going while there's momentum, and make note of all of the improvement opportunities identified. When the flow of ideas slows down, an effective retrospective review facilitator recaps the identified opportunities and solicits the group's input on which of those opportunities should be prioritized.

The team should focus on two to three improvement opportunities during the next phase (iteration, audit, etc.). This way, the team does not get distracted trying to remember a large number of behaviors to modify in the near future. Rather, the team stays aligned on their goals, including goals to support continuous improvement of the audit itself.

Note for clients: Retrospective reviews are a prime opportunity for your team to provide feedback to the auditors and improve your audit experience. It's also not uncommon for auditors to hold retrospectives with only their audit team (without the client). It's not that they don't value your team's opinion, but perhaps they hadn't considered soliciting your feedback, particularly if the retrospective reviews are only conducted at the end of the audit. In that situation, your team isn't likely to be audited again for a year or more, so they won't get to experience the benefits of the audit team incorporating this end-of-audit feedback. Instead, the feedback from the end of the audit will impact the next area under review by the audit team. Your feedback is still important, and I encourage you to ask for a retrospective review to be conducted and for your team to be included.

Furthermore, if the audit team doesn't plan to conduct retrospective reviews periodically throughout the engagement, I encourage you and your team to suggest them (or insist on them). This provides your team with the opportunity to influence a better experience during the audit rather than providing feedback that won't affect them. If something in the audit process could be improved, share the feedback!

The auditors can also provide feedback and suggest better ways of working during these retrospective reviews. They might suggest a modification that you and your team hadn't thought of. Help them create psychological safety in the retrospective by keeping the conversation focused on improving future activities ("What do we want to focus on improving?") as opposed to pointing fingers and focusing on past activities ("You did this and it didn't work at all!"). As with other concepts described in this book, your auditors may be new to performing retrospective reviews, or perhaps they're inexperienced in conducting retrospective reviews with the client. If this is the case, and your team has experience with conducting blameless retrospectives focused on improving work in the future, I encourage you to offer to facilitate the first retrospective review with the audit team, or provide them with the ground rules. This is another opportunity to influence a better experience for your team and further strengthen your relationship with your auditors.

CASE STUDY Fortune 100 Insurance Company

In an early attempt at Auditing with Agility, my team conducted a retrospective review when we were most of the way through the audit to determine how to become more effective through the end of the audit.

The team identified a number of improvement opportunities to incorporate during the rest of the audit, such as consolidating the team's questions for the external audit team and discussing them during the weekly meetings with the external auditors, when all relevant decision-makers were present (to increase consistency in feedback and direction given).

We implemented this practice throughout the rest of the audit and worked more efficiently. Some of the back-and-forth discussions from one meeting to the next and communication challenges of email chains were eliminated or greatly reduced. Had we not paused during the audit and instead waited until the end to solicit feedback, we wouldn't have experienced these benefits until a later audit (if at all).

In a subsequent experiment with Auditing with Agility, we leveraged a sprint-based audit approach. We held a retrospective review at the end of the audit's first sprint to identify what worked well (practices and behaviors to continue in the next sprint), as well as improvement opportunities (practices and behaviors to change in the next sprint).

We identified the following strengths: the continuous focus on value and reminders to focus on in-scope items (reducing scope creep), as well as the daily stand-ups with the collective team that we implemented partway through the sprint. We also identified challenges, such as excessive admin work from providing written status comments on each task card.

To reduce admin work, we decided to change the trigger for writing comments on the task cards. We started using them only when an impediment was present. This saved us time and frustration in subsequent sprints during the audit.

Real-Time Feedback Loops

Real-time feedback loops take the concept of retrospective reviews a step further by reducing the lead time between the need for feedback and the delivery of feedback. When auditors and clients collaborate closely and work together as one team pursuing a collective goal, real-time feedback often comes naturally.

Opportunities to apply agility to audit work through feedback loops are abundant, including opportunities outside of any specific audit engagements. For example, imagine that your team—a team of auditors, of audit clients, or of both—lacks clear visibility into what audit observation follow-up tasks are on the horizon. Without this visibility, team members run the risk of inadequately communicating the status of observation remediation (or acceptance). This could lead to observations remaining unaddressed longer than intended, or the need for last-minute, unplanned heroics on the client's part to quickly address the observation by the due date, or on the auditor's part to add validation work to their plate in addition to the audit work already in flight.

Following up on observations identified during an audit is an important activity and is required by the IIA. It doesn't make much sense to put in the work to identify gaps if nobody follows up to confirm the observations are addressed. The importance of following up on audit observations is further reinforced in Performance Standard 2500.A1 of the IIA's Professional Practices framework, which states the following: "The chief audit executive must establish a follow-up process to monitor and ensure that management actions have been effectively implemented or that senior management has accepted the risk of not taking action."[4]

To increase awareness of approaching follow-up deadlines, you decide to build a data visualization dashboard that will let auditors and clients see observation-related tasks coming due in the near future.* You could take a waterfall approach to this project. If that's the path you choose, you would plan out what the dashboard would look like and list out all the features to include. Then you'd build it and distribute it to the end users. The problem with this approach is that there is very little interaction with the end users. Even if you consulted them as you planned out the dashboard and listed out all the features they wanted, they wouldn't get to see it until the end. When you deliver it to them, you think your work is done. But what if you misinterpreted their requirements and delivered something different

---

* Some audit software tools include dashboards to show observation status. I included this example to illustrate the importance of feedback loops.

from what they need? Or what if you spent a lot of time developing a feature that they will rarely use?

This is a great opportunity to apply real-time feedback loops to a task that isn't directly tied to a specific audit engagement. To do this, you should identify the primary customers, or the intended users of the dashboard. Next, sketch out how the dashboard might look and what features should be included. Instead of diving in and building the dashboard at this time, solicit real-time feedback from the future users of the dashboard on which features they find most valuable (this anchors to valuing customer collaboration). With that insight from the intended users, you can now begin building the features that should bring the most value to those using the dashboard. Once the first version of the dashboard is ready, with some of the most valuable features implemented, it's time to solicit feedback again from the intended users. Ask the users to provide feedback on what was developed and to reevaluate the priority previously assigned to the remaining features to be implemented. Repeat this process until the dashboard is in a working state and meets the needs of the end users.

Establishing a culture of organizational learning and safety is a key to facilitating real-time feedback.[*]

Incorporating retrospective reviews and real-time feedback into the audit process creates a well-rounded feedback loop that drives more value into the audit process. Outside of specific audit engagements, auditors can also effectively apply these strategies to the annual/ongoing audit planning process by intentionally seeking feedback from the client throughout the year and adjusting the audit plan accordingly. Feedback loops also add value and efficiency to audit work beyond specific audit engagements and the audit plan.

> **CASE STUDY** Fortune 100 Insurance Company
>
> We incorporated feedback loops throughout one of our audits by intentionally soliciting feedback from the collective team of auditors and clients. In addition to conducting retrospective reviews at

---

[*] Establishing a culture of organizational learning and safety is further explored in Chapter 8. Another structured way to facilitate real-time feedback is by implementing stand-up meetings. Stand-up meetings are explored in detail in Chapter 7.

the end of each sprint and sending surveys to the client at the end of the audit, we also exchanged real-time feedback throughout the audit. Auditors and clients collaborated closely during the audit, which supported this exchange of real-time feedback. When issues arose, team members immediately gave feedback within the team, enabling us to pivot quickly to become more effective.

Since then, we've continued to embrace real-time feedback loops regardless of the audit delivery model. In one instance, our clients leveraged real-time feedback loops and asked if we could meet more frequently. This didn't require a specific forum like a retrospective review. The client took advantage of real-time feedback loops, and we're sure glad they did! Their idea let us all work more effectively by resolving roadblocks much sooner.

Chapter 7

Practices and Principles of Adaptable Auditing

Managing audit work in a way that enables response to complex, rapid change has been a popular topic in the internal auditing profession, beginning around 2017. This concept grows in popularity each year as organizations seek to understand and implement ways to stay ahead of the change curve by adding agility or adaptability to audit work.

Adaptable auditing focuses on improving the ability to respond to change and add flexibility into the audit process. While auditors can apply a specific framework, like Agile Auditing, to enhance the team's ability to respond to change, there truly is not one best way to practice adaptable auditing.

Incorrectly assuming something that works well in one instance will work well everywhere reaches beyond the auditing world. I recently experienced an example of this while traveling to conferences around the country to share my Auditing with Agility experiences. During these travels, I witnessed the ongoing struggle of getting luggage into the airplane's overhead compartment. The luggage needs to be placed a specific way (which can be different from one plane to the next) or it won't fit in the compartment. Some newer planes allow you to put your luggage in wheels-first but on its side. Others fit luggage wheels-first, but laying flat. Some older planes require roller bags to lay flat with the wheels to the side rather than wheels-first. Consider the situation where you're flying somewhere and the flight to your destination has two legs. During the layover between connecting flights, you switch planes. On the first leg of the trip, you must load your luggage one way into the overhead compartment (let's say wheels first). On the second leg, you're on a different plane. This time you need to load your luggage a different way— wheels to the side. The way of loading overhead luggage on the first flight worked well for that plane, but using the same approach on the second plane wouldn't have led to success. Instead, you'd get frustrated and feel glares from other passengers burning into you as you hold up the line. On this trip, you need to reassess your environment (the overhead compartment of both planes) and evaluate whether you need to make a change (loading the luggage differently on the second flight than you did on the first flight). Just as in this example of planes on the same trip with different overhead compartments, auditors and clients often need to pause and reassess the organization's operating environment to identify and respond to changes. Adaptable auditing lets you do this both while determining the schedule of audits to complete throughout the year and on each individual audit.

Just as we've done in previous chapters, we'll now walk through the various concepts of adaptable auditing from which you can choose when implementing Auditing with Agility:

- Value people over processes.
- Respond to change over strictly following a plan.
- Prefer face-to-face conversation over text-based, asynchronous communication.
- Promote sustainable work.
- Pursue simplicity.
- Leverage self-organizing teams.
- Organize stand-ups.
- Limit work in process.
- Reduce batch sizes.

Value People over Processes

As you learned at the beginning of this chapter, adaptability is based on the ability to respond to change. The concept of valuing people over processes helps auditors respond to change. Processes create structure and consistency, and most auditable units* are focused on specific processes or technologies. Therefore, it is still imperative for auditors to value processes. In addition to valuing processes, adaptable auditing teams place *more* value on people. Focusing on the people aspect *in addition* to the process side facilitates adaptability. It also increases employee engagement and builds stronger relationships. Auditors who operate with adaptability apply this value to the audit process itself.

In the absence of adaptability, auditors stay the course and execute the audit process without fully considering the client's perspective. Instead of focusing primarily on the process itself, adaptable auditors focus on valuing people and

---

* An auditable unit is a portion of the audit universe, which may be aligned to legal entities, business processes, technology platforms, etc. The audit universe represents everything the auditors have accountability to audit.

incorporating the team's perspectives to let the team pivot as needed to respond to changes rather than blindly sticking to a standardized process.

What could valuing people over process look like in practice? Here are a few examples:

- Staying connected with key stakeholders and leveraging their perspectives on what's valuable to the organization, modifying the audit plan or approach as necessary to stay aligned with the value
- Pausing intentionally throughout the audit to solicit input from the client on the remaining scope items and adjusting as necessary to account for changes in the environment
- Changing course when necessary to account for the client's input

Here's how the last example above might play out for you:

Auditor: We understand that a key control within the organization's payroll process is to ensure segregation of duties for changes made to the payroll application. For this, we need you to provide a system-generated list of users who can submit a change and a system-generated list of users who can approve a change. That's what you provided us when we tested this control the last time we audited this space.

Client: We can certainly get you both of those lists. I don't think those access lists will help you test the control, though.

Auditor: Oh? Please tell me more.

Client: Well rather than enforcing segregation of duties through access levels like we have in previous years, we recently built the control into the change pipeline. You see, the change pipeline is now configured to compare the ID of the approver on the change record with the ID of the person who submitted the change and to reject the change if the two IDs are the same. Everyone with access to the change pipeline has authority to approve a change, as long as it's not a change they submitted.

Auditor: That makes a lot of sense! So instead of the two access lists, we'll need to test this a different way. We'll need to see that the change pipeline permits a change when the approver's ID and the submitter's

ID are different from each other. We'll also need to see that the pipeline rejects a change when the approver's ID is the same as the submitter's ID.

Because the auditors valued the client's input, both the auditors and the client saved precious time. The auditors identified the need to deviate from the standard/previous request and modify it to account for changes in the control environment. Instead of inspecting irrelevant evidence that would likely have resulted in a potential audit observation that the team would later learn was not a risk or control gap at all, the auditor valued (and intentionally solicited) the client's input, resulting in a better understanding of the control and the evidence needed to test it. Valuing people over processes enabled the auditors to swiftly pivot earlier in the audit, saving valuable time.

Respond to Change over Strictly Following a Plan

Change occurs in today's environment faster than ever before. This pace of change affects many portions of the audit process, from the development of the overarching audit plan (impacted by organization-level changes) to the individual audit engagements (impacted by process-level changes). Let's first look at responding to change with the overarching audit plan, as that drives which audits the auditors perform and when they perform them. Then we'll explore adaptability through responding to change during individual audit engagements.

The audit plan is the schedule of audits to be completed in a given time frame. Internal Audit organizations, as well as other risk assurance functions, commonly build an annual audit plan based on the results of an annual, point-in-time risk assessment, auditing the areas of highest risk more frequently than those presenting a lower level of risk. Assessing the organization's risk once a year gives the auditors a great view of the risks the organization is facing *at the time of the assessment*. Risks can and do change more frequently than on an annual basis. Without intentionally revisiting the risk assessment throughout the year and adapting the audit plan accordingly, auditors may miss their chance to add the most value and audit what's currently most important to the organization.

Some organizations with heavy regulator oversight are required to review different parts of the organization on a specific cycle based on risk. For example, a highly regulated bank may be required to audit a high-risk process every year, while auditing a lower-risk process less frequently. Those organizations can still Audit with Agility. If the risk level of an area within the organization changes—let's say it increases—then the auditors and regulators will both want the auditors to audit the area that now poses a higher risk to the organization with a frequency aligned with the new level of risk. In reality, audit clients and the organization's stakeholders will want this as well. Conversely, if the level of risk posed by a particular part of the organization declines, it makes sense that the auditors should audit this area less frequently. This also aligns with a requirement to audit on a cycle that's driven by risk level, which is often prescribed by regulatory bodies.

Adding adaptability to the processes surrounding the overarching audit plan, an audit organization builds a plan, typically covering a year or a shorter time frame, and adapts the plan throughout the year to respond to organization-level changes like emerging risks. The risk assessment moves to a rolling, continuous risk assessment, with updates throughout the year to reflect current risk information. Continuous risk assessment facilitates more timely updates to risk ratings, which enables Internal Audit to provide assurance over the areas of increased risk sooner than if they had waited to make those adjustments (or waited to learn of the need to adjust the risk rating) on the annual cycle.*

To illustrate this, consider an audit plan that has audits A, B, C, and D scheduled to occur in the first half of the year. Through continuous collaboration between auditors and clients, as well as staying informed of risks impacting the industry, the need to do audit X arises. This could be due to a global pandemic that moved everyone to a work-from-home environment, which caused new risks to surface in a key business process. Or it could be due to a war in another country that raised concerns about the potential exposure to one of the countries in the organization's investment portfolio. Or it could be that the organization made a new strategic acquisition, introducing new risks.

Managing the audit plan with adaptability, the auditors make audit X a priority, and a previously scheduled audit (A, B, C, or D, whichever is now a lower priority than X) either moves off the plan or moves to later in the year to accommodate audit X.

Determining which audit to move in order to accommodate audit X requires auditors to consider a number of factors, which will be unique to each organization. Examples of factors to consider include:

---

* As mentioned in the Introduction, organizations can use artificial intelligence and machine learning to enhance audit processes. One use case is to leverage these tools in support of an adaptable audit risk assessment and planning process. Organizations can use these tools to identify current risks and predict upcoming risks and then pivot the audit plan accordingly. But remember, the focus should be on the process first and then on finding the right tool to support and enhance that process. Process first, then tools.

- Level of alignment of audits A through D with the organization's top objectives
- Value of (or risk covered by) audits A through D
- Audits in flight versus audits that have not yet been started

Now let's explore responding to change in an individual audit.

At times, the plan that was created at the beginning of an audit no longer reflects the most relevant risks and controls by the time the audit is finished. The risks and controls that were most important to achieving the organization's objectives when the audit began may no longer be the most important a few weeks or months later.

Teams that incorporate adaptable auditing intentionally pause throughout an audit to reevaluate the priority of the audit's scope or focus areas and adjust accordingly, embracing changes and pivoting their focus to the areas of greatest value. These teams embrace changes as necessary rather than staying the predetermined course.

It's easy to embrace changes early in the audit process, but what about when the need to change course arises late in the audit? It's important to embrace these late changes as well. Essentially, auditors and clients operating with adaptability embrace changes, regardless of when the team identifies the need to change.

Changing when needed, even late in the audit, is incredibly important in situations where risks are emergent, processes are in flux, and new information flows quickly. Teams that quickly and intentionally pivot when needed help the organization make sound business decisions and achieve their overarching goals, even when this pivot occurs toward the end of an audit.

At the core of adaptable auditing is the ability to adapt to change. The client's needs may also change throughout the year or during the course of an audit. As the team identifies the need to change, they should ensure high levels of transparency to impacted parties (auditors, the client, and other stakeholders).

Failure to embrace changes may lead to outdated results that do not constitute delivery of value. This often contributes to strained relationships between auditors and the client. If the client doesn't see the value in the auditors' work, the relationship can slip from those of trusted advisors to the dreaded corporate enforcers.

Responding to changes as the need arises and making those decisions visible to impacted parties help to preserve and nurture the relationship between auditors and their clients.

> **CASE STUDY** Anywhere Real Estate Inc.
>
> Using the traditional waterfall audit approach, Anywhere Real Estate's Internal Audit team faced the challenge of "scope lock," where the team was locked in to completing the audit program set forth at the start of the audit. At times, the team would get a few days into an audit and realize that some of the items on the audit program* weren't as much of a priority as something the team just learned about (that wasn't on the audit program). Moving to a more adaptable approach, including backlog refinement and being intentionally open to change, enabled the team to become more risk responsive.[1]

Prefer Face-to-Face Conversation over Text-Based, Asynchronous Communication

Before the COVID-19 pandemic, face-to-face, in-person communication was the most effective way to communicate during an audit. Since 2020, face-to-face communication has taken on a new meaning. While many organizations continue to open their offices and welcome associates back into corporate buildings, not all of those organizations are back to full-time in-person work experiences . . . and many never will be.

In today's environment, where working remotely or in a hybrid environment is common, organizations have had to open their minds about the best methods of effective communication. While in-person, face-to-face conversations are still incredibly effective, as these conversations can occur with any level of formality and nonverbal forms of communication are more clear, there are other ways to effectively communicate.

Email has historically been the go-to method of communicating during an audit. Email's trail of documentation reduces the chance of the client successfully denying that they provided specific evidence or communicated specific information, but we're moving beyond the "us" versus "them" working model, right? As our working model evolves, so should our preferred methods of communication.

---

* An audit program articulates the procedures the auditors will perform during an audit.

When moving toward adaptable auditing, face-to-face methods of communication should be our go-to. But what does that look like in a hybrid or remote work environment? It looks like this:

- In-person fly-bys (stop by the other person's desk for a quick question)
- In-person meetings (everyone in a conference room or huddled around a dry-erase board)
- Virtual fly-bys (brief video calls for a quick question)
- Virtual meetings (preferably with cameras on to facilitate nonverbal communication as well)

Of course, face-to-face communication in today's environment is not limited to the four instances listed above. The emphasis here is on tailoring the communication method to fit the specific need. Keep lines of communication open and adjust formality as needed. These types of communication help build rapport and strengthen relationships way more than receiving a faceless email. They're also more likely to facilitate faster responses. It's easy to ignore an email or let it get lost in the barrage of emails received every day. When someone swings by your desk or calls you on a video call, you're more motivated to get them what they need. It's also pretty hard to ignore an incoming video call (particularly if your status in your team's collaboration tool indicates you're available) or to ignore someone physically standing at your desk.

Promote Sustainable Work

When audit organizations leverage an annual risk assessment and planning process, where the audit plan for the year is laid out and committed to at the beginning of the year, the end of the year (or the end of the annual period) can get pretty busy. If audits take longer than expected and work gets pushed back to later in the year, the work tends to pile up into the last few months of the year. At that time, the remaining audits on the annual plan need to be delivered, and there's usually more work than originally planned. Documented approvals are needed to deviate from the original plan and to move audits from one year's plan to another.

Some audit organizations have scorecards that emphasize the importance of completing all of the work committed to in the annual audit plan. When those audits are not delivered by the end of the year, some executives or higher-ups might view this as a failure to meet expectations. This creates the need for year-end heroics by the auditors and the clients to deliver the committed audits, which results in an unsustainable pace and burnout.

By the time the year ends, the auditors and clients are burned out and need a long break to recover and get ready to begin the following year's audit plan. This in turn leads to a slower start in the beginning of the following year, further contributing to an end-of-year time crunch. The problem never seems to resolve itself and oftentimes worsens. Adding adaptability during the annual risk assessment and planning process helps alleviate this problem. Using a rolling audit risk assessment and planning process enables flexibility and adaptability—and thus sustainability. In a rolling audit risk assessment and planning process, the audit organization either maps out and commits to the work for only the next quarter (or whatever length of time is most appropriate for that organization), or it maps out the work for the entire year, commits only to the work to be completed in the next quarter, and intentionally revisits the rest of the year's plan throughout the year prior to committing to the next quarter's work.

Under this structure, the audit group has intentional points during the process to assess the current environment, such as the risks impacting the organization at that time, the organization's current key initiatives, and the current state of the audit organization (impact of turnover, audits not completed on time, audits completed early, etc.), and commit to a reasonable amount of work targeting the areas of most value to the organization. This reduces the likelihood of committed work piling up at the end of the year, thus reducing the need for year-end heroics. Without the need for year-end heroics, everyone enjoys a much more sustainable workload.

Pursue Simplicity

Simplicity is essential to adaptable auditing. It is not uncommon for auditors to try to audit everything, evaluating every possible risk and every control within a process. Not only does this go against the concept of promoting sustainable work, but it also doesn't provide the most value to an organization. Nor does it facilitate the ability to pivot and adapt. Audit teams that remove wasteful practices through pursuing simplicity are better able to respond to changes.

The IIA's International Standards for the Professional Practice of Internal Auditing (the Standards) require internal auditors to exercise due professional care.[2] The IIA further clarifies in supplemental guidance that "due professional care does not imply infallibility. Therefore, internal auditors are not expected to give absolute assurance that noncompliance or irregularities do not exist."[3] As such, auditors must challenge themselves when identifying an audit's scope.

Instead of auditing everything, auditors should focus on the areas of most value or highest risk to the organization. To help transition from the tendency to over-audit, auditors can refine the audit's scope to focus on what needs to be audited while excluding things that don't add value. Here are a few examples of questions auditors can ask when simplifying an audit's scope (a similar version of some of these questions appeared in Chapter 5):

- What has to go right for the organization to be successful?
- If a gap in this control is identified (i.e., the control is not designed or operating effectively), how big of an impact would it have?
- Would stakeholders be intrigued by or value feedback on this control, or would they shrug it off?
- What value will the organization get from knowing whether or not this control is effective?
- How much does the organization depend on this control's effectiveness to achieve its objectives?
- What is the worst thing that would happen if this control was not effective, and could that affect the organization's ability to achieve its objectives?
- How can the process or controls be improved in order to improve the organization's outcomes?

By asking these questions and refining the scope, teams are better positioned to pivot when necessary. Teams that maintain simplicity in the audit's scope and reduce the effort spent on activities that do not add value are more nimble than those who do not. For example, if a team asks what value the organization can expect from knowing whether a control is effective, and the answer is "no value," then the control should not be audited. The team should focus on something that *will* provide value to the organization instead.

In addition to applying this principle to an audit's scope, organizations leveraging adaptable auditing also identify how to work more efficiently. It is important to simplify the audit process while still complying with professional auditing standards. Just as auditors provide a fresh perspective to the areas they're auditing, pursuing simplicity may require a fresh perspective to evaluate existing audit practices to identify areas that could be simplified or eliminated. Simplifying these processes allows auditors to spend more time adding value to the organization than working through specific audit steps that are outdated or inefficient. If they're spending less time executing outdated and inefficient tasks, they are better positioned to adapt to changes along the way. Audit clients also spend less time on these less effective items too, creating a win-win situation.

To help auditors identify opportunities to simplify, consider audit tasks that don't clearly tie into the group's goals or intended outcomes. Really seek to understand why they're doing these tasks. Do these tasks directly or indirectly support achievement of the audit engagement's objectives or adherence to the Standards? If not, should they still be completed? If they do support achievement of the engagement's objectives or adherence with the Standards, is there perhaps a better or more efficient way to accomplish the same thing?

Another helpful question to ask is what the team could not do during an audit while still accomplishing the engagement's objectives and complying with requirements. Auditors are uniquely positioned to help the client pursue simplicity as well. By being independent from the process or product under review, auditors often don't have the context as to why the client started doing certain tasks or performing controls in a specific manner. By asking the elementary questions (there are no dumb questions!), auditors help the client challenge old and outdated ways of working and trade them for more efficient or effective ways of accomplishing objectives.

Examples of these kinds of questions include "what prompted you to do this control in this fashion?" and "if you had a magic wand and could do your work differently to accomplish the same goal, what would you do or how would you do it?"

Reducing the client's workload makes it easier for them to adapt to changes as well. Circling back to the primary problem introduced in the Introduction of this book, auditors who help their clients accomplish their goals more efficiently or effectively, removing unnecessary steps and simplifying the process along the way, are likely to experience stronger working relationships with their clients.

> **Note for clients:** Just as the auditors bring a fresh perspective to your work, you can also provide a fresh perspective to the audit process. That perspective can help your auditors in the same way that theirs helps you. Ask the elementary question about why the audit team does certain things. You'll either get a deeper understanding and appreciation of the importance of specific audit tasks, or you'll help your auditors simplify their process and increase efficiency. That's a win-win!

Leverage Self-Organizing Teams

A self-organizing team is a team that does not depend on one single person to dictate how best to accomplish the team's goals.

Advantages of self-organizing teams are plentiful. The primary advantage is the ability to pivot. Other benefits include:[*]

- Increased efficiency
- Better alignment of work with skills
- Better alignment of work with interests and development goals
- Better alignment of work with capacity

Self-organizing teams have a collective commitment to achieving the team's goals. Self-organizing teams are not incentivized solely on individual achievement. Nobody wins if one team member finishes their work early and others struggle to complete their tasks, thus jeopardizing achievement of the team's collective goal. Instead, all of the team members win when the team's goal is met. This collective commitment encourages team members to jump in and help each other out where needed, thus increasing adaptability. It also encourages team members to seek help earlier rather than spinning their wheels trying to solve a problem in isolation, focused only on achieving their individual goals.

Because of the early visibility into challenges and available team members jumping in to help alleviate those challenges, self-organizing teams keep work moving forward with more velocity than teams that are not self-organized, especially when faced with unexpected challenges. This also shifts individual motivators ("I need to keep my knowledge to myself to prove my value and focus on getting my own work done before anyone else finishes") to team motivators ("My team is running into delays that are threatening achievement of our goal, and I have the knowledge and resources to help. Don't worry, friends, here I come!"). This environment, which embraces sharing knowledge, further increases the value each team member brings to the organization and their ability to adapt to change.

In an audit-specific context, collective commitment to a team goal also helps remediate scope creep. Because auditors have a tendency to want to audit everything, scope creep (doing work beyond the scope of the audit) often rears its ugly head. The collective commitment of a self-organizing team combats scope creep

---

[*] Although the benefits of self-organizing teams also align with value-driven auditing and integrated auditing, I placed this concept in the chapter on adaptable auditing, as the primary benefit of self-organizing teams best aligns with adaptable auditing.

because everyone is aligned on achieving the team's goal. When a self-organizing team identifies scope creep, the team members exhibit adaptability by quickly pivoting away from the work that expands beyond the intended scope and back *toward* the work that matters.

Consider this scenario. During a payroll audit, the team's goal is delivering value by providing assurance that the payroll process's controls are effective. The team has identified the process's key controls and evaluates their effectiveness. While testing a control, one of the auditors identifies another control that wasn't previously identified as key to the payroll process.

The self-organizing team considers whether to add this control to the audit's scope by determining whether including the newly identified control helps achieve the team's goal (delivering value by evaluating the effectiveness of the payroll process's key controls). If the additional control test helps the team achieve their collective goal, then it is added to the audit's scope (adapting the scope to accommodate). If it does not directly support the team's collective goal, or if testing that control to determine effectiveness won't deliver additional value to key stakeholders, then it is not added to the audit's scope.

In addition to collective commitment, self-organizing teams should collectively possess the skills necessary to complete the audit. When transitioning to adaptable auditing, it is recommended to include someone who is familiar with professional auditing standards in the team membership. This provides a resource within the team to evaluate whether practices with which the team experiments comply with professional auditing standards. This further reinforces the psychologically safe environment necessary for innovation by equipping the team with the necessary knowledge (and often solutions) to meet professional obligations. If the audit scope includes both operational and technology components, the team should include auditors with expertise in operational auditing and technology auditing. Each team member brings a unique skill set to the team. Collectively, the team is strengthened by combining these diverse skill sets and is better prepared to respond to unknown information and change as it is encountered throughout the audit. Rather than depending on individuals outside of the team, the team depends on its own members, who are committed to the audit's objectives, which reduces wait times.

Adaptable auditing leverages self-organizing teams that also include members of the client's team familiar with or accountable for the area under review. Auditors cannot effectively provide assurance over a specific process or product without a certain level of knowledge of that process or product. Including the client in the team provides the process-specific or product-specific knowledge necessary for the audit work. This characteristic of self-organizing teams promotes upskilling of all team members by working together and filling in knowledge and skill gaps. When auditors and the client work so closely together, some people in the organization might question the audit team's ability to maintain independence and objectivity. In short, auditors can operate in this fashion while being independent and objective primarily by maintaining decision rights, as well as through separate organizational reporting lines. We explore this in much greater detail later on.

Another characteristic of self-organizing teams is high levels of collaboration. This applies both among the auditors and with the client. All team members, including all auditors assigned to the audit as well as members of the client team involved in the process or product under review, should be included in all phases of the audit to maintain a consistent flow of information. This positions each auditor on the team to be able to complete work in support of the team's goal rather than working in a silo, focused only on the work assigned to them. This also positions the client to effectively and efficiently complete the client tasks in support of the collective team's goal (providing evidence, discussing potential control gaps, creating awareness of control gaps with executives, etc.). This also facilitates adaptability by facilitating well-rounded knowledge throughout the audit rather than in pockets, which better positions the team to pivot as needed (e.g., if someone is out unexpectedly). By including audit clients in the self-organizing team, auditors and clients work together more frequently, facilitating real-time feedback. That real-time feedback enables teams to adapt as needed to address the feedback.

One practice commonly leveraged on self-organizing teams is the pull method of assigning work (versus the push method). Under the waterfall approach, traditional audits use the push method of assigning work. With this method, the auditor in charge assigns work to each staff member. This is typically done at the beginning of the fieldwork stage of an audit (the stage where control testing occurs). While this creates clear expectations for each audit staff member on what they are expected to do during fieldwork, it often results in workloads that don't align with staff members' capacity, passions, development goals, or skill sets. Often, one auditor will finish their assigned work earlier than expected, while another is behind schedule. When the work has already been assigned out (or *pushed* to the staff), it isn't easily reassigned.

Conversely, the pull method of assigning work empowers the audit team to *self-assign* work. Instead of the auditor in charge telling each auditor what work to complete, team members identify work that aligns with their capacity, interests, development goals, and skills. If the auditor has time off scheduled later in the week, they can self-assign a control test that is more straightforward or will require less effort to complete. On the other hand, if another auditor on the team has a lot of capacity this week, they can self-assign a control that takes more effort to complete. They can also self-assign work that is engaging and interesting to them. If an auditor is really interested in learning more about how the client ensures payroll calculations are accurately processed, that auditor can assign that control to themselves. Or if a more junior auditor wants the opportunity to complete a task typically completed by someone with more experience, they can take on that work. That doesn't mean that the less glamorous tasks aren't completed. The team is aligned on a collective goal of delivering value to stakeholders, so even the less exciting tasks get completed. Besides, what one person may see as boring, another may see as an exciting new opportunity!

This empowers team members to take ownership of the overall outcomes of the audit, as well as the tasks each individual completes. This collective commitment, paired with the collective knowledge of the team, better positions the team to be flexible and to quickly respond to changes.

CASE STUDY Fortune 100 Insurance Company

In the first sprint of one of our Auditing with Agility pilots, the auditor in charge assigned the work for the duration of the sprint to the audit staff at the beginning of the sprint. Some of the auditors finished their assigned tasks before others. It was difficult to reassign some of the work from one auditor to another to balance out the workload because the remaining tasks were at varying stages of completion.

In the second sprint, we decided to take a different approach. Instead of the auditor in charge assigning all of the work at the beginning of the sprint, each auditor assigned work to themselves, and they only took on what they could reasonably complete in a few days or a week. This left some tasks unassigned, which was quite unusual for the team and created a bit of unease with the auditor in charge. Inevitably, we found ourselves again in the situation, where some of the audit staff completed their work before others (due to a number of factors including competing priorities and the complexity of each control). This time, however, it was much easier for the auditors with capacity to find available work—they simply looked at the task board, found a task card that wasn't assigned to someone else, and tagged themselves on the card, thus claiming it for themselves. Empowering the team to self-assign tasks was initially uncomfortable for the auditors, particularly for the auditor in charge, as it differed significantly from the normal workflow they had each grown accustomed to over the years. We acknowledged the apprehension while leaning in to the change, knowing that this audit was all about experimenting and learning. We had no idea whether self-assigning tasks would be successful, but we were all willing to give it a try. Although we were a little uncomfortable and clunky at first, the team appreciated the ability to select their own tasks, better aligning their assignments with their capacity and development goals.

As we continued to implement Auditing with Agility on subsequent audits, we continued to mature in how we leveraged self-organized teams. To enable more fluidity of staff between audits, we moved our task board from Microsoft Planner to Jira to facilitate making our work visible. With Planner, we had a board for each audit, and you could only see the task cards for audits to which you were assigned (this was likely a limitation of the way I set up Planner and used it rather than a limitation inherent to the tool). Switching to Jira, I created a board to house tasks for all of our audits. Everyone on the team could see all of our audits and the tasks associated with each audit. We also added cards for follow-up activities related to audit observations to ensure we didn't lose track of them. This also enabled us to give them the attention necessary to "monitor and ensure that management actions have been effectively implemented or that senior management has accepted the risk of not taking action," as required by the IIA's Performance Standard 2500.A.1.[4]

There are some tasks that require little to no knowledge of the area under review to complete (e.g., uploading the audit report to the audit tool after it's been issued). When someone finished their work early and found themselves with unplanned capacity, they could explore the Jira board and pick up available tasks, even on audits to which they weren't originally assigned. Using Jira also enabled me to break down the team's work into weekly iterations, which helped us prioritize work for the week and focus on those items. I also began using the reporting and dashboard functionality within Jira. These functions visualize how the team is progressing each week and whether or not we met our weekly commitments.

Organize Stand-Ups

Another practice used in adaptable auditing, which we discussed briefly in Chapter 6, is a daily stand-up. Daily stand-ups are meetings held each day, typically only fifteen minutes in length, with the collective team (including auditors and the client) to ensure the team knows what they are going to accomplish that day and to identify and resolve roadblocks. Auditors can also leverage these meetings to ask follow-up questions and request additional information. By including all the necessary client contacts in the stand-up, there isn't a need to go ask someone else and get back to the team. The knowledgeable parties are all present, so answers to questions and requested documentation are typically provided during the stand-up, thus increasing efficiency.

Stand-ups are also useful for discussing and beginning to align on potential audit observations. Similar to the initial audit meeting, involving all auditors assigned to the audit and all clients who work on the controls under review enables knowledge sharing, which can reduce duplicative efforts and duplicative requests from the auditors. The goal is to keep the stand-up to the fifteen-minute timeslot, so if topics arise that require additional dialogue, the team reconnects outside of the stand-up, typically with the same group of attendees.

Stand-ups also provide the ability to pivot quickly to change. After all, if you meet every day and know what everyone is doing, challenges, changes, and new information bubble up quickly. The team is all together in one space, ready to face the challenge and pivot as needed.

What does a stand-up look like in practice? One way to conduct an effective stand-up is to have each team member briefly share what they accomplished since the prior day's stand-up, as well as what they plan to accomplish before the next stand-up. Stand-ups create an opportunity for team members to mention obstacles and escalate any impediments to the team. The team can then take action to remove the impediment.

Consider the situation where the impediment to completing a control test is that the auditor is waiting for the client to provide additional information about some of the evidence they previously provided. If the client is in that stand-up, they can provide the necessary information at that time, immediately removing the impediment. If the client is not included in the stand-ups, the team can connect with the client once they're made aware of the impediment and help to get the information necessary for the auditor to complete the control test.

To keep the stand-up within the fifteen minute timebox, it's helpful to table items that need additional discussion to the end of the stand-up. Some teams prefer to schedule the stand-ups for thirty minutes each day, reserving the first fifteen minutes to discuss daily accomplishments and commitments, as well as identify impediments, and using the second half of the meeting to address anything that needed further discussion.

This differs from the traditional audit approach where an auditor is assigned a specific control and works independently to complete that control, connecting with the assigned point of contact as needed. If the auditor asks a question related to their assigned control, and the assigned point of contact doesn't have the answer, the point of contact has to go find the right contact, get the answer, and then circle back with the auditor. This can take a few days to complete. What this auditor learns about their control is not typically shared with the other auditors on the team.

In some cases, controls are closely related, and without stand-ups, the audit team may miss out on an opportunity to share knowledge and improve adaptability. Additionally, two auditors working on closely related controls might ask the same question of their points of contact. Nobody has time for duplicate efforts or answering the same question twice. Even if stand-ups only include the auditors, the team can still experience greater efficiency and increased knowledge sharing.

Stand-ups encourage collaboration within the audit teams because the teams aren't testing controls in silos, oblivious to what their teammates are doing. Someone may share that they're waiting for the client to answer one of their questions. Another auditor in that meeting may have learned the answer to the question from testing their own control. By communicating the impediment to the entire audit team, other auditors can step forward and remove the impediment if they have what's needed to do so.

When auditors and the client conduct stand-ups together, they may also use that time to communicate audit observations that they've identified. Because those observations are discussed in daily stand-ups or as follow-up to daily stand-ups, the results communicated at the end of the sprint, iteration, or audit are not a surprise to anyone.

Note for clients: As someone who interacts with auditors and other risk functions or assurance providers, it is understandable that when these parties come to perform their work, the additional work for you and your teams is largely unplanned work. Even though you are aware the audit is coming, it is difficult to account for the day-to-day impact to your team's commitments. To ease this burden, find ways to incorporate the audit team and audit work into the way you typically manage your team's work. If your teams hold daily stand-ups (or stand-ups held at a different frequency), invite the auditors to participate. This will help integrate the audit work into your team's daily work, making it both visible and actionable. It's also likely that the auditors don't know how to run effective stand-ups, particularly if they are early in their Auditing with Agility journey. Since your team is experienced in managing work this way, I encourage you to invest the time to teach the auditors what you know about running effective stand-ups. It's likely your team will experience benefits during the current audit, as well as in subsequent audits.

CASE STUDY Fortune 100 Insurance Company

In one of our first attempts at incorporating Auditing with Agility, the audit team held daily stand-ups that supported flexibility and reinforced the urgency and priority of the audit. These stand-ups enabled the team to

- seek and address feedback continually,
- shift available resources to tasks that needed attention,
- share knowledge among the team, and
- change testing procedures on the fly to adapt to stakeholder feedback and needs.

Limit Work in Process

Limiting work in process (WIP) places limits on how much work can be actively worked on at once. It reduces the amount of putting down a task to shift to another and then shifting focus back to the original task. Limiting WIP reduces multitasking and time lost to context switching. In addition, it creates space (or slack) on the team so that they have the cognitive load available to pivot or adapt to changes. Instead of dividing the work upfront and each team member going off and doing their work with their head down, focused on completing their assignments ("I know what I need to do, so I'm going to put my head down and get it done!"), teams that limit WIP create minute breaks where team members can reassess the remaining tasks and shift their focus as needed. When we have a bunch of tasks in process concurrently, it's difficult to identify opportunities to shift focus and adapt as needed. That's because each team member is focused on their own tasks that are in process. When teams limit WIP, as a task is finished, the team member who finished the task evaluates the remaining tasks to determine which to begin next. This creates an opportunity for the team member to determine whether there is a need to change. The team member takes this opportunity to ask themselves whether they learned anything new or if anything has changed that would necessitate changing the audit. Thus, limiting WIP increases the team's adaptability.

WIP limits can be enforced per person or by the total number of tasks in process. When using a task board with columns representing each workflow step, teams can also place WIP limits on each column of the board. Once the limit is reached (e.g., an auditor has the maximum number of tasks somewhere between "to do" and "done"), no new work can be started until the WIP is reduced below the limit. Using WIP limits at the individual level, a team may limit the amount of tasks each auditor may have in process to a certain number of tasks. Let's say, for example, the limit is three tasks. Once an auditor has three tasks in process, they cannot take on a new task until one of the in-process tasks is complete. Once one of those in-process tasks is complete, the audit goes back under the WIP limit. To illustrate with another example, consider a WIP limit on the number of items in the peer review or the auditor in charge review column. When the WIP limit is reached, the team swarms around the bottleneck to get the pending items reviewed. In this case, the bottleneck is too many items waiting to be reviewed. Clearing the bottleneck gets the review queue back under the WIP limit, thus getting things closer to delivery of value.

CASE STUDY Fortune 100 Insurance Company

One audit when we leveraged Auditing with Agility was a high-profile project with a lot of attention from our organization's key stakeholders and a tight completion time frame. My team focused on limiting WIP by limiting the number of audits the team was on concurrently. The team was composed of dedicated resources that were focused primarily on this engagement. This differed from our normal operating model, where each audit staff typically worked on anywhere from two to six audits at once. During this audit, the team's priority was crystal clear, so we spent less time reevaluating priorities than is typical when juggling multiple projects. In addition to limiting the number of audits the team was on concurrently, we also limited WIP within the audit. The staff only took on one task (e.g., control test) at a time. As someone finished a task, they could quickly jump on to another task. This increased the team's adaptability.

We then expanded our use of WIP limits on subsequent audits. For example, team members self-assigned tasks and took only what they could work on and complete within a reasonable time frame, which was typically one or two tasks at a time. This made tasks more visible, as we could easily see tasks that hadn't moved from In Process to Under Review on the task board. With visibility into tasks that were not progressing, we targeted these items in our stand-ups to remove the impediment that prevented the task from moving forward. We learned that some of the impediments were work that was not represented on the task board. "I haven't been able to work on this task because I've been working on X." We then evaluated whether X was something that would help us achieve our collective goal for the audit. If it was, we created a card for X. If it wasn't, then the associate shifted their focus from X to the tasks related to this audit.

By taking on tasks only when a team member could work on and complete the task (i.e., limiting WIP), we achieved a more consistent alignment of work with availability and a greater ability to respond to change. Instead of each person having an individual lot of tasks to complete, they chose what to work on based on their availability. If they had time off scheduled and only a day left to work on something before being off, they chose a task that would take a day or less to complete. This left tasks available for someone else who had more capacity to take on work, resulting in fewer delays due to a pile-up of tasks in one person's queue. This also reduced the amount of multitasking the team dealt with. Instead of switching between a lot of different tasks at once, each auditor focused only on one or two tasks at a time. This created more opportunity for the team to adapt as needed throughout the audit.

Reduce Batch Sizes

In manufacturing, a batch is a group of goods produced at one time. In technology, a batch is a group of jobs that are processed at once. In an audit, the batch is a unit of value delivered. In the waterfall approach to auditing, the batch is large, with a single batch consisting of the following:

- Identifying all key risks and controls in scope
- Testing all in-scope controls
- Discussing and aligning on conclusions, including audit observations, with the client
- Communicating all conclusions

With the waterfall approach, the team cannot move to the next step (testing all controls) until the prior step is completed (identifying all controls), making it rigid and adverse to change. Plus, value is not delivered until all of the above items are complete. Large batch sizes typically bring with them lots of work in process.

In the previous section, you learned that high levels of WIP lead to multitasking and context switching, translating to wasted time. High levels of WIP can also impede a team and prevent them from adapting to change. More WIP is not your goal. Neither are larger than necessary batch sizes. In adaptable auditing, batches are smaller. For example, a batch could be a single control conclusion. In this instance, the following occurs:

- Identify a key control.
- Test said control.
- Discuss and align on the conclusion from testing said control, including audit observations, with the client.
- Communicate conclusions on said control.

Similar to the first example where the batch size is larger, the team cannot move to the next step until the prior step is completed; however, end-to-end, this is a much smaller unit of work, which takes less time from start to finish. This means value is delivered sooner and there are more points at which the team can evaluate the work and adapt to change as needed.

Rather than delivering all the value at the end of the audit, value is delivered incrementally, with much of the value being delivered earlier in the audit. This helps the client keep their own batch sizes smaller.

Ultimately, the global goal—for both Internal Audit and the client—is helping the organization achieve its objectives. If the client receives all of the audit conclusions and audit observations at once, they may try to address the audit observations all at once, which is a large batch size. This could cause the identified risks to remain open until all audit observations are addressed. When small batches are used, conclusions are delivered to the client incrementally, making it easier for the client to address gaps in small batches. This often leads to risks being addressed sooner, and addressing risks sooner helps the organization achieve its objectives. Additionally, since WIP may be limited, the client may be more efficient in addressing the risks. Helping the organization achieve its objectives is aligned with both Internal Audit's goal (aligned with the definition of internal audit) and the client's goal.

Management addresses gaps

Risks addressed

Organization achieves its objectives

Audit and Management achieve global goal

Audit conclusions delivered

Figure 7.1: Benefits of Small Batches in an Audit

Toward an Audit Transformation

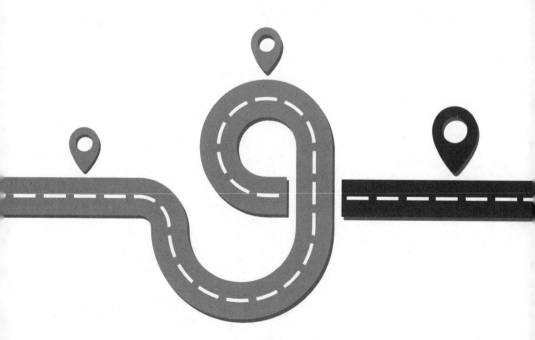

Chapter 8

Making the Transition to Auditing with Agility

The time to move to Auditing with Agility is now. Organizations can no longer apply a static audit approach to dynamic processes. Risks now change with radical velocity, and auditors need to keep up with, if not stay ahead of, the risk curve. Audit organizations that don't change their approach will quickly find themselves providing less value and losing significance.

Anthony Pugliese, president and CEO of the IIA, reinforced the urgency as follows in the June 2022 edition of *Internal Auditor Magazine*: "As we look to our future, we must resist the urge to rest on our laurels. In an era of constant disruptive innovation, complacency is the greatest threat to success."[1]

How to Start the Transformation

A key theme appearing throughout this book is that of a mindset shift. Moving beyond the days of auditing with a strict, one-size-fits-all approach to auditing with flexibility and customization requires a new mindset for both auditors and the client.

As with any change, there will be varying levels of support for the change to working in the ways described in this book, both from the client and from auditors. Some individuals will be supportive and will want to help lead the charge to Auditing with Agility. Others will likely dig in their heels and resist the change. The rest of the organization will fall somewhere between those two groups. Those who are most supportive are more open-minded about the change and may see it as an opportunity to be thought leaders and learn through experimentation. Start your journey with these highly motivated individuals. Give them a safe space to experiment in and learn from these better ways of working, and they'll stay encouraged throughout the journey, even when facing adversity.

What about those who aren't quite as excited about the change but don't completely oppose it? These are your first followers. Show these individuals the progress those who started the journey made. Show them the success as well as the safe environment that's open to experimentation and learning. Pair them up with some of the highly motivated individuals so they can experience the journey themselves. Once they do, they too will become highly motivated individuals. Then give them the space and support to run with it.

> **Note for clients:** The concepts outlined above apply both to auditors and clients. If your team is excited about improving their audit experience, let your auditors know that you're all in. Find those on your team who can champion this journey and create excitement among others.

You can apply the same concept of starting with motivated individuals and supporting and empowering them to specific audit assignments as well. Doing so further supports transitioning to Auditing with Agility. By aligning work with individuals' interests, you'll be leveraging highly motivated individuals who look forward to the work they'll be doing.

For example, if an upcoming audit will focus on a particular area of the organization that Auditor A is passionate about or interested in learning more about, include Auditor A on that audit. Or if someone is really interested in learning how to identify key risks and controls, empower them to take the lead on those tasks within an audit. If this is their first time taking on this type of task, they likely won't get it right the first time. Empower them to give it their best. Support them by providing feedback and encouraging them to learn and grow from it. Align work with interests, build projects around motivated individuals, and support and empower them. Motivated, supported, and empowered individuals become change champions.

Now you've identified the team members who are ready to embark on this journey. Let's get them started by getting them in line for the Auditing with Agility smorgasbord!

The Auditing with Agility Smorgasbord

The key to Auditing with Agility is selecting the best approach for a specific situation and desired outcomes, adjusting along the way as needed. Operating under an edict that all audits must be performed as a waterfall or that all must be performed in sprints is not operating with agility and may not accomplish your goals. Instead, you should apply an agile mindset and use the Auditing with Agility smorgasbord concept.

The options are laid out for you in the previous chapters. Now you get to select the practices you want to experiment with. Will it be dividing your scope into prioritized areas of focus to drive more value into your work (Chapter 5)? Will you pair that with feedback loops from Chapter 6 to further integration between auditors and the client? And what about reducing batch sizes from Chapter 7 to increase adaptability? The choices are endless. Determine what you're trying to accomplish with the audit—what are your desired outcomes?—and then select the practices that will best help you achieve those outcomes.

For example, let's say on a particular audit, the auditors and their clients agree that what's most important for the audit is getting results into the client's hands as soon as possible. Both auditors and clients also want to see increased efficiency during the audit process. Now that it's clear what the team wants to accomplish, let's figure out what elements of Auditing with Agility the team could incorporate on this particular audit to achieve those outcomes. To get results into the client's hands sooner, the team could choose to implement feedback loops or to deliver value frequently through iterations or sprints. There are a number of items to select from to achieve the outcome of increasing efficiency of the audit process, including the following:

- Increasing visibility
- Intentional collaboration
- Working together daily
- Integrated planning
- Feedback loops
- Responding to a change over strictly following a plan
- Pursuing simplicity

After evaluating the options available to them, the team chooses to start by implementing X, Y, and Z, promising to analyze the results at the end of the audit and tackle new strategies in the next audit.

Setting Yourself Up for Success

Now that you have a strong understanding of the mechanics and mindset needed to achieve the incredible benefits of Auditing with Agility, you'll want to understand how to create an environment that empowers your teams to experiment with Auditing with Agility and supports them along the way. You want to set them up for success. Here's how you do that.

Culture of Organizational Learning and Safety

When implementing Auditing with Agility and changing to a new way of working (after decades of using the same method on every audit), you must cultivate a culture of learning and safety. This is a concept borrowed from DevOps.[*]

To understand a culture of learning and safety, let's first explore what this type of culture does not look like. In the absence of a learning and safety culture, when something goes wrong, team members tend to sling accusations at each other and seek a scapegoat. This can cause people to hide their failures for fear of being blamed or chastised. This type of culture also often discourages innovation, as innovation inherently brings the risk of failure. Failure leads to finger-pointing in a culture without safety.

In the context of an audit, it may look something like this. When a quality review of the audit organization identifies instances of noncompliance with auditing processes, blame is assigned to an individual (or spread like peanut butter across the whole audit organization) and more red tape (e.g., additional approval gates) is added to the audit process.

In a culture of learning and safety, instances of nonadherence to the audit process are examined as part of the quality review to identify opportunities to improve the process (improved training, useful templates, updated requirements or procedures, etc.) rather than to blame or punish an individual or the entire audit organization.

For the client, the absence of a learning and safety culture looks like leaders who fear audit observations. Even when the observations are accurately portrayed in the audit communication, these leaders resist including the observations in the final audit communication, or they try to soften the language or downplay the risk of the gaps articulated in the audit report. Rather than focusing on remediating control gaps that exist in the environment, the client spends energy fighting the audit observations for fear of retaliation by their leaders.

Now consider a different culture, one where learning and safety are the focus. In this culture, the same situation looks like this: leaders seek to understand audit observations and help auditors ensure accuracy and clarity of the contents of the audit report, which communicates audit observations to senior leaders. In this cul-

---

[*] See the Appendix for more on the Three Ways of DevOps.

ture, the client helps deliver the message with the auditors rather than working against them. The client does not fear retribution from their leaders because of the content of the audit report. The client seeks to learn from the experience and improve their processes, building in safety to prevent future recurrences.

In this culture, the client does not withhold information from the auditors; rather, they are forthcoming with known gaps and share their plans for addressing their observations. The client works closely with their auditors to help them assess key controls, recognizing that it is better for the client and Internal Audit to identify gaps that exist than it is to keep them hidden from the auditors and wait for them to manifest into something catastrophic.

Furthermore, when organizations cultivate a culture of learning and safety, the client proactively reaches out to their auditors when they're implementing new processes or tools to get the auditors' perspective and advice on potential risks and useful controls the client could enact. This further reinforces safety by building in controls and mitigating risks during the implementation of these new processes and tools rather than after the fact. Auditors are happy to provide these consulting services, as they align with the shared goal of helping the organization achieve its objectives.

Using another audit-related example, the absence of safety in an organization's culture can lead to finger-pointing, unproductive arguments, and assigning blame when a team misses an audit deadline.

> **Auditor in charge (to audit staff):** "You didn't finish your testing on time!"

> **Audit staff:** "The client took too long getting me the evidence I needed in order to do my testing!"

> **Client:** "Well, your request wasn't clear, so how did you expect me to get the right evidence to you?!"

And before you know it, the client and the auditors are adversaries fighting each other rather than working together to help the organization.

This situation plays out differently in a culture of learning and safety. When learning and safety are core tenets of an organization's culture, audit team members work together to understand what events and circumstances led to the missed deadline. The entire team, including both auditors and the client, participates in this activity to ensure multiple perspectives are shared. The team stays focused on identifying solutions (forward-thinking, learning) rather than dwelling on the breakdown (backward-looking, blaming). This shift from dwelling on the past and placing blame to focusing on solutions and learning opportunities encourages the intentional risk-taking necessary for innovation. When the team no longer fears punishment or shaming when failure occurs, they begin to see these instances not as failures, but as experiments and learning opportunities.

In a science lab in highschool, students perform experiments with the intent to learn. If an experiment doesn't yield the expected or intended result, students are encouraged to learn from the experiment and share their learnings with others. The emphasis is on the learning process rather than the outcome itself. This mindset of learning from experiments has use far beyond the highschool science lab. It also belongs in organizational cultures.

> **CASE STUDY** Fortune 100 Insurance Company
>
> Recall from Chapter 2 where I shared my experience working within a culture of learning and experimentation. I shared that toward the end of one of our Auditing with Agility experiments we reverted to old ways of working (the auditor versus auditee operating model) when compiling the final audit report and soliciting input on the overall audit opinion. Unfortunately, this pitted my clients against myself and my team, replacing our fun, in-this-together relationship with an adversarial confrontation. Fortunately, this was a temporary switch. Throughout the audit, we created a culture of learning and safety that fostered taking risks and learning from failures. Because of this, the reversion back to old ways of working and adversaries was temporary. We quickly gave each other grace, learned from the misstep, and moved forward together—stronger than ever.

Transforming Local Discoveries into Global Improvements

In addition to creating and maintaining a culture of learning and safety, organizations embracing Auditing with Agility also transform local discoveries into global improvements. This practice encourages organizations to transcend individual learnings to drive broad-reaching improvements. One method of expanding the reach of individuals' knowledge is to share learnings from training or conferences. Sending everyone in an organization to a conference can get pretty pricey (registration fees, flights, hotel, meals, etc.), and realistically, most organizations won't authorize that cost. Instead, organizations could invest in sending one to a few associates to a conference and reserve time for them to share what they learned with the rest of the team or organization. Each individual who attended the conference not only learns through attendance but also solidifies their understanding by sharing with the rest of the team—and they're helping to upskill their teammates as well.

Another way to transform local discoveries into global improvements is through sharing knowledge on an audit. Through the practices described in previous sections, local knowledge becomes team knowledge. Instead of each auditor conducting their own control walkthroughs independent of each other, multiple auditors (if not all auditors working on the audit) attend walkthroughs or working sessions, even if the primary topic is not directly related to their control. There's a good chance the knowledge gained in that working session or walkthrough will be helpful for everyone in attendance. This also becomes useful in the event someone needs to be off of work unexpectedly. That knowledge from the control walkthrough isn't only in that one auditor's brain or on their laptop. Others on the team were in attendance and now have the knowledge necessary to step in and complete the control test. This can also be achieved through shared documents and collaboration tools. Maintaining a shared document where the team collects their notes gives all of the auditors access to valuable information about the area under review.

The key here is to encourage knowledge sharing. A culture of learning and safety is imperative for this. Without a culture of safety, auditors may resist sharing their knowledge for fear of losing their value to the team ("If I am the only one who knows about X, then the team depends on me and needs me!"). Instead, with a culture of learning and safety, the team will see the value in sharing their knowledge with others ("I learned this and I'm going to increase my value to the team by sharing it with all of them!").

Reserving Time to Create Improvements and Learning

Many organizations, including audit teams, require a minimum number of training hours each year. In fact, the IIA's Attribute Standard 1230 states that "internal auditors must enhance their knowledge, skills, and other competencies through continuing professional development."[2] Auditors who hold certain designations are required to obtain a minimum number of continuing professional education (CPE) credits annually. For example, practicing auditors who hold the Certified Internal Auditor designation offered through the IIA are required to obtain forty hours of CPE each year,[3] and those who earned the Certified Information Systems Auditor designation offered through ISACA must obtain 120 hours of CPE each three-year reporting period.[4]

This sounds great on the surface. Who doesn't want to continually get better at what they do or make their work easier? Unfortunately, auditors tend to get so caught up in the daily work of meeting with the client, evaluating evidence, reviewing workpapers, and socializing audit observations that they often let professional development fall to the bottom of their priority list. When the year starts coming to an end, auditors get emails from certifying organizations (the IIA, ISACA, the Project Management Institute, etc.) notifying them that CPE requirements are due in a few weeks. Then it's a race against the clock to find any free or low-cost CPE courses to meet the minimum annual requirement. Taking this approach, it's not likely that those available courses align incredibly well with the auditor's development needs. They've missed an opportunity to invest in themselves.

Similarly, auditors get so caught up in daily work that they may forget to improve upon the daily work itself. They can get bogged down in administrative or manual tasks without fully knowing why the tasks should be completed. Perhaps these tasks were important at one time, but do they still really need to be completed? If yes, could they be performed differently to create efficiencies? Without intentionally improving daily work, auditors can get farther and farther behind, spending less and less time doing work that truly adds value.

This isn't isolated to auditors; the client isn't immune to this, either. The client gets focused on maintaining their products or business processes, which can cause them to deprioritize professional development activities and activities associated with improving daily work.

To break out of this downward spiral, organizations need to intentionally reserve time to learn and improve daily work. This can be accomplished in a number of different ways, including blocking and protecting calendar time for learning, teaching, and improving daily work. The key here is in protecting the time set aside for these activities. It is easier to protect the time if the entire organization reserves the same date/time on a consistent basis (e.g., every Tuesday afternoon from one o'clock to three o'clock), and leaders set the expectation that that time is to be used only for learning, teaching, and improving daily work. This time can be incorporated into monthly team or department meetings as well.

Of course, you don't strictly need a calendar-driven trigger for these activities. Instead, organizations can reserve time at the end of each audit, or at other trigger points in the audit, to create improvements or to learn. This can be part of a retrospective review performed at the end of each audit or each sprint. Learning activities should also show up on the team's task board. By including the assignment to intentionally improve daily work on the team's task board, the team proritizes improving daily work during that week (or whatever time period the team uses to prioritize and deliver work).

Adding intentionality into the mix, as well as the expectation that time reserved for learning and improvement be respected and not prioritized over, organizations can watch their associates grow and flourish in their roles. Associates will be better prepared for the next step in their career. They will spend less time getting bogged down with work that doesn't make sense or adds little value; instead, they'll improve the work, resulting in increased effectiveness and efficiency.

CASE STUDY Anywhere Real Estate Inc.

Anywhere Real Estate's Internal Audit organization periodically sets aside two-week sprints, during which a team of auditors focuses solely on department-level initiatives identified to improve the department's processes, deliverables, etc. During this time, the team completes no audit work. Reserving and protecting this time as a sprint enables the team to focus on key initiatives without getting distracted by other priorities.[5]

In this chapter, we've explored how to make the transition to Auditing with Agility. We've also seen case studies—in this chapter and sprinkled throughout the previous chapters—illustrating elements of organizations' unique journeys to Auditing with Agility. As you embark on your own journey, I want to leave you with a few more case studies. You'll see that each journey is unique. Yours will be too.

CASE STUDY Barclays

During her time at Barclays Bank, former Chief Internal Auditor Sally Clark sought to optimize and improve the audit function and improve collaboration within the audit team at Barclays. At the time, she had observed that many audit team members had stopped having verbal conversations with each other during the audit process and had resorted to keyboards and fingers tapping away, with emails often only traveling a couple of feet across the office.

As Sally relayed to me in our interview, she invited Jon Smart, who led Barclays's Ways of Working team at the time, to speak to the Internal Audit team about how he was introducing better and more agile ways of working in the technology functions at Barclays. Sally quickly realized that Internal Audit might be able to harness some of these practices into audit work to achieve better outcomes.

Her team approached this transformation in a very simple way to start. They took time to understand the Agile principles, considering what they could do from within and what external help they needed as well. They also investigated how they could set themselves up for success. Starting with some purist approaches and principles, the entire audit team was trained in better ways of working. Sally offered some members of the team the opportunity to step out of their daily work to become part of a centralized team focused on adding agility to audit work. She also hired external Agile coaches.

Through a culture of continuous experimentation and learning, Barclays Internal Audit implemented various practices from each of the three components of Auditing with Agility: value-driven auditing, integrated auditing, and adaptable auditing.

They implemented value-driven auditing by delivering audits in two-week sprints. They also used a physical task board to increase visibility of the audit, with columns representing stages of the audit workflow, including To Do, Doing, and Done. As a result, audit observations were communicated to audit clients earlier.

Aligned with the core component of adaptable auditing, Barclays Internal Audit team held daily stand-ups. All team members participated in these daily stand-up meetings, where the team discussed progress, roadblocks, and potential audit observations. This enabled the early surfacing of either problems that might slow down the audit or observations to share with audit clients. More experienced auditors listened to the less-experienced auditors, offered advice, and helped to remove impediments.

The team implemented integrated auditing as well, by inviting the audit clients to weekly stand ups and, at times, physically wheeling a task board directly to where the clients were located. At the end of each two-week sprint, the audit team held retrospective reviews, during which the team looked back over the previous two weeks and assessed what had gone well and what could have gone better.

The Barclays Internal Audit team saw incredible results by leveraging these practices. Right away, they experienced productivity gains of between 10% and 20% in terms of delivery. But beyond that, they realized the culture changes that had come with the approach were way more than they could have hoped for:

- Junior auditors enjoyed daily interaction with managers.
- Underperformers were identified quickly and were helped to improve their performance.
- The noise levels in the office showed that there could be a real buzz at the stand-ups as the teams discussed progress.
- The teams proactively identified ways to enhance the audit process.

One example of process improvements the auditors identified was with regard to report writing. Instead of one person pulling together the findings, rewriting them, and wrapping them in a report, the auditors compiled the report with the whole team present. This reduced the time to get a report done from ten days to three hours, which was incredible![6]

CASE STUDY Capital One

Capital One is a Fortune 100 financial services company headquartered in McLean, Virginia. Capital One's Internal Audit organization, which has approximately 300 auditors, implemented Auditing with Agility concepts like self-organizing teams (adaptable auditing) and prioritized areas of focus (value-driven auditing). As a result, the shift "is allowing internal audit to engage management earlier in the audit process and create more transparency in all aspects of how it delivers work."[7]

CASE STUDY Fortune 500 Property and Casualty Insurance Company

A Fortune 500 property and casualty insurance company also began leveraging the core components of Auditing with Agility and experienced great results! Prior to incorporating Auditing with Agility, this organization's twenty-three auditors struggled with rigid audit scoping, tended to create a plan and execute all of it rather than adjusting efforts as needed to accommodate changes, and experienced misalignment between risks and audit activities. Between 2020 and 2022, they began providing real-time feedback to the client (value-driven auditing)—increasing collaboration by identifying key risks, controls, and testing procedures together with the client (integrated auditing)—and incorporating flexibility into scoping decisions (adaptable auditing). By leveraging Auditing with Agility, the organization's Internal Audit organization reduced the average length of audits by thirty-one days, driven primarily by a reduction in time spent testing and reporting results. The Internal Audit director at this organization attributes this to being nimble in scope (adaptable auditing) and collaborating more closely with the client (integrated auditing). In addition to shorter audit cycles and more timely delivery of results, the audit team has felt more connected to the work, and the work is more closely aligned with the organization's key risks and priorities (value-driven auditing).[8]

Chapter 9

Overcoming Challenges to Transformation

When implementing radical changes to a tried-and-true process, you can expect some challenges. Even when the benefits are clear, humans are creatures of habit and naturally gravitate to what's comfortable and consistent. This section addresses some of the challenges you might face when transitioning to better ways of working and provides actions teams can take to overcome these challenges.

Get Comfortable Being Uncomfortable

Auditors are often known as being "process people." Many find comfort in understanding how a process works and in following a consistent process to complete their work. Auditors have leaned on the waterfall framework and traditional project management practices for decades. This is likely why many in the auditing profession gravitated to Agile Auditing as a substitute framework. Frameworks are comforting. There are step-by-step instructions explaining how to perform the work and rules that tell us whether we're performing tasks correctly.

For example:

- A sprint should be no longer than four weeks in length.
- The time allocated to planning a sprint is limited to two hours of planning for each week in the sprint.
- Stand-ups occur daily and last no longer than fifteen minutes.

It's particularly comforting for auditors to have a familiar, well-laid-out plan for conducting an audit because auditors are typically not experts in the area they're auditing. Auditors are experts in risks and controls and in the audit process. Switching up the audit process itself and modifying how things get done can definitely cause some apprehension for auditors. That's why they tend to gravitate toward replacing one framework (waterfall audit process) with another (strict Agile Auditing framework).

To be clear, I'm a big fan of Agile Auditing and the benefits of delivering in sprints. I'm not a fan of replacing one problem with another. One of the key problems with the waterfall audit process is that it does not allow for the flexibility needed to drive the most value in today's ever-changing environment. While Agile Auditing adds flexibility, making a switch from all-waterfall-all-the-time to all-sprints-all-the-time will likely land us right back where we started: applying the same approach to every audit in every situation, assuming that one size fits all when it really doesn't.

Instead of replacing one problem with another, Auditing with Agility embraces an ever-evolving toolkit from which auditors and the client can choose the best tool or approach to fit a given situation and desired outcomes. Because each audit is unique (people, processes, and technologies differ from one area under review to another), the audit approach should be customizable in order to deliver the most value and achieve desired outcomes in each unique situation.

So while a strict framework is comfortable to both auditor and the client, rigidly following a framework won't always yield the best results. That's because the focus is on executing or "doing" the framework rather than on the outcomes we're using the framework for (e.g., improved working relationships, delivery of value sooner, improved ways of working, and increased ability to respond to change). Besides, comfortable is boring and outdated. Let's get comfortably uncomfortable. That's where growth thrives.

Note for clients: Audit clients have also grown accustomed to being subject to audits. Clients expect to spend time with the auditors in the beginning of the audit to give the auditors the information and documentation they need. Then the auditors will go away for a few weeks, leaving the client to focus on their own work. Later in the audit process, the auditors return to present the results. Knowing what to expect in an audit is comforting. It may be unnerving when the auditors show up and tell you they're totally revamping the audit process. As uncomfortable as an audit may have been, at least you knew what to expect from the process itself. Now what? Will you be guessing throughout the entire audit? What is the new framework the team will be using? These concerns are valid. You're not alone. A 2018 survey by the IIA revealed that "overly traditional expectations of executive management are a roadblock to agility."[1]

Rest assured, though, that this new way of working is indeed a better way of working. While the auditors may not set out a specific step-by-step process for you to follow on the audit, you will be brought along the entire way. The collaborative nature of this way of working encourages you to ask questions, contribute your unique perspective, and be part of the audit rather than having the audit be something you're subjected to and something that's done to you. On the surface, the new approach may seem ambiguous and haphazard, but I assure you, this time it's substance over form. Parts of the new way of working will seem familiar to you (helping the auditors understand your process, fulfilling documentation requests, and receiving results). The parts that are less familiar to you (working together to identify the most effective way to test controls, maintaining high levels of collaboration throughout testing, and receiving results way earlier in the process) will add value for you and your team.

Change the How, Not the What

I often get asked if Auditing with Agility changes the essence of what auditing is. No. I'm not suggesting that the purpose of an audit, or the purpose of the profession, for that matter, be thrown out and rewritten. In fact, I'm not suggesting any changes in *what* auditors do. What I am suggesting is that *how* auditors perform their work needs an upgrade.

The IIA defines internal auditing as "an independent, objective assurance and consulting activity designed to add value and improve an organization's operations. It helps an organization accomplish its objectives by bringing a systematic, disciplined approach to evaluate and improve the effectiveness of risk management, control, and governance processes."[2] Nothing about this changes when auditing using the methods described in this book. What auditors do does not change with Auditing with Agility. How they go about their work is what radically changes—for the better.

Complying with IIA Standards*

The IIA maintains a set of standards that outline requirements to guide the professional practice of internal auditing. Many Internal Audit organizations adhere to these standards, developing policies and procedures to facilitate adherence with them.

When incorporating Auditing with Agility, you are likely to encounter concern from your peers, leaders, or team with regard to adhering to the standards. During my personal journey, I was often asked, "Won't we be failing to comply with the standards if we work this way?" Like the challenges we've explored previously, this is a challenge you can overcome. This section highlights the standards that commonly come into question, and it focuses on the IIA's Standards.[†]

After reading this section, you'll be able to evaluate the professional auditing standards your team uses as its guiding star, and you can identify ways to incorporate these practices without violating those standards.

Standards Requiring Independence and Objectivity

When auditors and the client work together so closely during an audit, it's only natural to question the auditor's independence and objectivity. After all, the IIA's Standards require independence and objectivity. Specifically, Attribute Standard 1100: Independence and Objectivity states, "The internal audit activity must be independent, and internal auditors must be objective in performing their work."[3] There are a number of other internal auditing standards defining requirements related to independence and objectivity, namely 1110, 1112, 1120, and 1130. Clearly these concepts are of paramount importance to the Internal Audit profession. So how do auditors maintain independence when working so closely with the client?

Independence is still preserved primarily through organizational reporting structures (e.g., the audit organization reports to the board of directors or a

---

* This does not constitute official guidance from the IIA. I've thoroughly reviewed IIA Standards, and this book has undergone peer reviews. I have applied these practices as an audit practitioner without violating IIA Standards. Based on peer reviews and my experience with these practices as an audit practitioner, I feel comfortable that the practices as described in this book do not violate IIA Standards.

† It's important to note that at the time of this writing, the IIA is in the midst of updating these very standards to guide auditors and their organizations through the practice of internal auditing in the ever-evolving global landscape. The refresh of these standards is exciting, as updating the standards to be more relevant in today's environment is aligned with one of the goals of Auditing with Agility: updating audit practices to account for today's environment, as well as tomorrow's.

committee of the board and does not report through management). Objectivity is preserved through that independence, as well as through retention of decision rights. When determining the scope of the audit, what to include and what to exclude, it's imperative that the auditors retain decision rights. Auditors must not ignore their professional judgment when making these decisions, nor must they defer decision-making regarding audit activities to the client. By intentionally driving high levels of collaboration between auditors and the client, the auditors will be better positioned to make well-informed (not influenced) decisions. Objectivity is further maintained, as the auditors are not involved in designing the controls and are not involved in performing the controls.

Furthermore, the IIA issued guidance clarifying that "independence does not imply isolation. There must be regular interaction between internal audit and management."[4] Not only does this support movement away from an adversarial mindset, but it also emphasizes the importance of collaboration between auditors and their clients. In essence, while auditors may be worried about violating their profession's standards when working in this fashion, the standard-setting body actually *encourages* this way of working.

Performance Standard 2240: Engagement Work Program

Internal auditors must develop and document work programs that achieve the engagement objectives.

2240.A1 – Work programs must include the procedures for identifying, analyzing, evaluating, and documenting information during the engagement. The work program must be approved prior to its implementation, and any adjustments approved promptly.[5]

You might be thinking, "Ah, but this standard requires an approval gate. We're required to approve the work program before we implement it! That means we can't work in sprints or add agility by welcoming change throughout the audit, right?" Not necessarily. This standard does indeed require approval of the work program before the team executes the actions outlined in it (e.g., approve the controls to test before actually testing the controls). What this doesn't say is that you have to have it all figured out for the entire audit before you can move to the next stage. If you're running an iteration-based audit, you'll gain approval of the work program for each iteration before you start testing the controls in that iteration. Or if you're focusing on being more open to change throughout the audit (regardless of whether you're delivering in iterations), pausing intentionally throughout to see if the scope outlined in the work program still makes sense, that doesn't mean you can't get approval on the work program in the beginning (we all want to make sure we're directionally correct before getting too far). You can then gain approval on each of the subsequent changes to the work program. Since you're leveraging higher levels of collaboration, even within your own team, you're including the individual with approval authority in the periodic scope reevaluations, so getting that individual's approval is quick and straightforward.

Performance Standard 2100: Nature of Work

As you've learned throughout this book, the nature of audit work does not change in Auditing with Agility. How that work is accomplished changes, but the work itself does not. Therefore, if you were complying with this standard before implementing these improved ways of working, and you don't change the nature of the work (the "what") when you incorporate Auditing with Agility, you wouldn't have changed your alignment with this standard.

Standards Regarding Planning the Engagement

2200 – ENGAGEMENT PLANNING
Internal auditors must develop and document a plan for each engagement, including the engagement's objectives, scope, timing, and resource allocations. The plan must consider the organization's strategies, objectives, and risks relevant to the engagement.

2201 – PLANNING CONSIDERATIONS
In planning the engagement, internal auditors must consider:

- The strategies and objectives of the activity being reviewed and the means by which the activity controls its performance.
- The significant risks to the activity's objectives, resources, and operations and the means by which the potential impact of risk is kept to an acceptable level.
- The adequacy and effectiveness of the activity's governance, risk management, and control processes compared to a relevant framework or model.
- The opportunities for making significant improvements to the activity's governance, risk management, and control processes.[6]

These standards require auditors to consider a number of items when planning an audit engagement. Many of these required considerations necessitate the need to have a certain understanding of the area under review. Based on the required considerations in 2201, who in the organization is best positioned to help the auditors understand these items? The client is. Whoever on the client's team is closest to the area under review is likely going to be a great asset in helping the auditors understand the strategies and objectives of the activity under review, how the key controls are performed, the most significant risks in the area under review and how those risks are managed, and the key governance processes within the area under review.

Performance Standard 2330: Documenting Information

In Chapter 5, you learned that Auditing with Agility encourages auditors to value actionable insights over extensive documentation. You may be thinking, "This is exactly what I was worried about. Do you see now why we can't adopt these practices while complying with the standards? The standards require documentation!" Don't worry; I hear you. Let's take a closer look, starting first with the standard:

> Internal auditors must document sufficient, reliable, relevant, and useful information to support the engagement results and conclusions.[7]

The requirement is to document information in support of audit results and conclusions. That information must meet the following criteria:

- **Sufficiency:** Documentation must include enough information to support the results and conclusions to enable someone else to reach the same conclusions.
- **Reliability:** Information documented must be obtained through appropriate techniques, such as inspection of evidence, direct observation, and corroborative inquiry.
- **Relevancy:** Information documented must pertain to the audit objectives and conclusions.
- **Usefulness:** The documented information must align with the business value/goal of helping your organization achieve its objectives.

Now it's clear what you need to document to meet the requirements set forth in the Standards. What about valuing insights over documentation? Aren't these two ideas in conflict?

No. The Auditing with Agility concept in question represents prioritization of value, not a binary choose-one-and-not-the-other directive. Valuing actionable insights over extensive documentation means that you value both items. You just don't lose sight of wanting to deliver actionable insights for the sake of perfecting the supporting documentation. Nowhere in the Standards does the IIA require perfect documentation. Perfection or extensivity is not one of the four elements of documentation required in this standard.

In summary, Auditing with Agility may initially seem to be in conflict with Standard 2330 on the surface; however, a closer examination of the requirements of this standard and the intent behind the Auditing with Agility concept in question reveals that these two concepts are not mutually exclusive.

Standards Regarding Communication of Results

2400 – COMMUNICATING RESULTS
Internal auditors must communicate the results of engagements.

2410 – CRITERIA FOR COMMUNICATING
Communications must include the engagement's objectives and scope as well as applicable conclusions, recommendations, and action plans.

2410.A1
2410.A1 – Final communication of engagement results must, where appropriate, contain the internal auditors' opinion and/or conclusions. When issued, an opinion or conclusion must take account of the expectations of senior management, the board, and other stakeholders and must be supported by sufficient, reliable, relevant, and useful information.[8]

You may find yourself faced with the following objection: "Reporting in this way (iteratively or throughout the audit) doesn't comply with the Standards. We have to have one report at the end of the audit." This is a misconception. Nothing in the Standards requires you to issue only one final report at the end of the entire audit. The Standards require internal auditors to communicate results, and they specify information that must be included in those communications. The Standards don't even specify that it has to be a *report* at all.

2420 – QUALITY OF COMMUNICATIONS
Communications must be accurate, objective, clear, concise, constructive, complete, and timely.[9]

We've already explored the objectivity in prior sections. The key element here is timeliness. Using the methods described in this book, one of the outcomes is getting value (audit results) into the client's hands sooner. This standard requires timely communication of results, so rather than failing to comply with the Standards using these new ways of working, you'll actually be even more aligned with them!

The application of the techniques described in this book does not prohibit you from adhering with the IIA's Standards. In fact, in some cases these practices enable you to adhere more closely with the Standards than with current practices. Instead of viewing these better ways of working as an impediment to adhering with the Standards (or viewing the Standards as an impediment to implementing better ways of working), they may indeed be a solution resulting in *better* alignment between practices and standards.

CASE STUDY Fortune 100 Insurance Company

Reflecting back on my team's experience during one of our Auditing with Agility experiments, I realize that on the surface, it appeared to be all rainbows and unicorns. While there were many more positive results from implementing these better ways of working, the successes didn't come without challenges. One challenge we faced was a fear that working in new ways would violate professional internal auditing standards set forth by the IIA.

We overcame the fear of violating professional auditing standards by expanding our team's membership to include someone well versed in the IIA's Standards. This individual was a member of our Internal Audit Professional Practices team. He provided insights to us along the way and answered our questions related to professional auditing standards and helped us stay compliant with the Standards while adopting these newer ways of working. The team progressed from saying "we can't do this without violating the Standards" to instead asking "what can we do to work in this new way while meeting the requirements of the Standards?"

Workload/Backlog Management

The way in which the audit team's workload and assignments are managed can also benefit from an uplift in the form of agility. Typically, audit teams think about an audit as an end-to-end project, with a number of controls to be tested and tasks to be completed before the end of the audit. Auditors are assigned to different audits that are in process simultaneously. There is a lot of work in process, and it's unclear how much work the team can accomplish in a given period of time. There are also likely pockets of unbalance in workloads (some auditors are overwhelmed, while others are underwhelmed and looking for more work). This can result in teams overcommitting and underdelivering.

Auditing with Agility teams think of audit work as more of a product (value through assurance and risk insights) rather than a bunch of projects. Key stakeholders get more value from the results auditors deliver than they do from audit projects consistently meeting internally set deadlines. Meeting deadlines and staying within budget are important; however, anchoring back to Internal Audit's definition, an audit is "designed to add value and improve an organization's operations. It helps an organization accomplish its objectives by bringing a systematic, disciplined approach to evaluate and improve the effectiveness of risk management, control, and governance processes."[10]

Staying on budget and meeting deadlines are not mentioned in that definition; however, adding value is. Auditors value deadlines and budgets. On the other hand, auditors who want to revolutionize their way of working, become strategic differentiators, and increase their value to the organization tend to value delivering assurance and insights even more.

Teams can accomplish this through managing a backlog of work to be completed. Certain tools can be helpful in managing a backlog, but here we will stick to the concept and process. Chapter 5 introduced some of the tools that can facilitate better workload/backlog management, specifically those related to increasing visibility of audit work.

A backlog is essentially a list of tasks that need to be completed. Examples of such tasks in an audit include the following:

- Scheduling a meeting with key points of contact to identify key risks, controls, test procedures, and evidence
- Testing a control
- Scheduling time with the client to discuss the audit's status
- Documenting an audit observation

- Drafting the audit report
- Updating risk assessment documentation

Clearly, this is nowhere near an exhaustive list. Rather, it shows the wide variety of tasks in a typical audit backlog. An audit may have hundreds of tasks. The number of tasks in an audit depends on the size and complexity of the audit, as well as the granularity with which tasks are broken down. The audit team documents tasks for a given audit or the selected area(s) of focus in the audit backlog.

Backlog management practices teach audit teams to better predict what they can accomplish and deliver each week. They also facilitate better delivery of value to stakeholders through a process called backlog refinement, where teams review the backlog each week to determine where the team should focus their efforts during the week. This encourages the team to consider the tasks in the backlog and challenge whether those tasks support the team's goal (providing value-driven assurance and insights), as well as to identify which are more of a priority to complete than others.

During these backlog refinement sessions, the team commits to tasks to be completed in the upcoming week. This typically takes some time to fine-tune. It's not usually clear in the beginning how much work the team can accomplish in a given week. Since the audit team has historically estimated the amount of work the team can accomplish throughout the entire three-plus-month audit (with varying levels of accuracy), it's not always easy to translate those estimations into one-week increments. That's okay. Don't give up. Make the best estimate you can without spending too much time trying to be incredibly precise.

During the next backlog refinement session, see how close you were and try estimating again. Eventually, the team will get better at estimating how much effort each specific task requires (each task will have its own estimation—one type of control test is typically more involved than another, lending itself to a greater effort needed to complete it), as well as how much the team can realistically accomplish in the given time frame (typically one week). The team will be able to adjust for constraints on capacity during that time frame, such as planned time off and conflicting commitments.

Continuing with the payroll audit example we've visited throughout the book, consider the audit team that is focusing on the application used to process payroll. The team met with key points of contact and knows the key controls applicable to this area of focus. Tasks in the audit backlog at this point in time could include the following:

- Access control design test
- Access control operating effectiveness test
- Application change management control design test
- Application change management control operating effectiveness test
- Application interface control design test
- Application interface control operating effectiveness test
- Application patch management control design test
- Application patch management control operating effectiveness test
- Schedule time with the client to review remaining areas of focus
- Draft final audit report: scope section
- Draft final audit report: audit objectives section

Again, this is not an exhaustive list and should not be used to develop the scope of an audit in practice. It should be used only for illustrative purposes to understand backlog management.

Taking into consideration the audit team's capacity during the upcoming week (consider planned time off, holidays, other work commitments outside of this particular audit), the audit team collectively determines which tasks can realistically be completed in the upcoming week. Those items are moved into the week's backlog, with the items not selected remaining in the overall audit backlog. As the week progresses, the audit team works on the tasks selected for completion that week. Any prioritized work that is not completed during the week is revisited as part of the next week's backlog refinement session. If the team completes all of the prioritized work before the end of the week, auditors revisit the overall backlog and pull tasks forward into the current week's backlog.

> **Bonus**: If the client uses backlog management practices to manage their own work, auditors can get their audit tasks incorporated into the client's backlog. The clients will be delighted! Here's why: If the client uses backlog management techniques, they plan out the work they're completing over a given time period, typically one week. If audit work (e.g., requests for documentation or information) are not included in the client's backlog, the audit work becomes unplanned work for the client. This jeopardizes their ability to fulfill the obligations they have prioritized for the week. Seeing this from the client's perspective, they committed to delivering a certain number of items this week and then

the auditors came along and added unexpected work to their plate. Now they won't be able to deliver what their leaders are expecting. That doesn't help strengthen the relationship between auditors and the client. In fact, it likely deteriorates it. So, if the client uses backlog management practices, auditors should integrate the audit work into those practices. This enables the client to accommodate audit requests without jeopardizing their own commitments and results in more clarity on when the auditors can receive requested information and documentation. It also strengthens the relationship between auditors and the client.

Note for clients: If you manage your work using a backlog and conduct backlog refinement sessions, talk to your auditors about this. Even if they choose not to manage their work in the same manner, there's a good chance you can influence them to incorporate their requests of your team into your backlog management process. Help them understand how they can help you. Show them how your team plans out their work for the upcoming weeks. Show them how they can incorporate audit requests into your team's backlog and explain to them the benefits, both for your team and theirs. Their requests are more likely to get the necessary attention from your team in a timely fashion. Your team can also better plan for the audit work, which means team members can make appropriate commitments (rather than overcommitting and underdelivering). Partnering in this way helps strengthen the relationship between your team and the audit team, which is a win-win.

Put Processes and People before Tools

When transitioning from one way of working to another, teams often fall into the trap of focusing on tools over processes and people. Tools like Jira boards, artificial intelligence, machine learning, or the latest and greatest audit software built for auditing in iterations can support a solution (like Auditing with Agility); however, tools in and of themselves are not solutions. A tool without a process or people is a wasted investment. Organizations with a tool-first mentality must later retrofit a process into the selected tool and then must train the people on the tool and the new process. Likewise, organizations that jump to the latest tooling trend (like AI and ML) without sufficiently evaluating its use case will find themselves paying for a tool or developing a tool with many failed attempts at achieving value from it. For example, the organization that dives head first into artificial intelligence to enhance audit work without a clear plan and process for effectively leveraging that technological advance will be disappointed by the lack of direction and tangible outcomes from the investment.

It should be the other way around: invite and cultivate a mindset of agility and value-driven work, develop a process to bring agility to life and drive value to the forefront of the work, and then leverage tools to support the process. Tools do not drive the work; people do. People drive value-added work through processes. Those processes can be enhanced or facilitated through the right tools. Focus first on improving the process rather than implementing the latest and greatest tool.

Exile Edicts and Mandates

Another common (and flawed) approach organizations take when shifting to better ways of working is to issue an edict that a specific process is to be applied to all audits. This is common with organizations looking to "become Agile Auditing shops," as these organizations typically mandate that all audits be performed using a strict Agile Auditing framework. While this might work in the instance where the work is unchanging and predictable (some compliance audits or SOX audits), the majority of audit work is dynamic and less predictable. As such, doing effective and valuable work may look different from one audit to the next. In one instance, following a strict Agile Auditing framework will yield the best value. In another instance, forcing delivery in sprints could be disastrous.

Let's explore some of the factors that are needed to successfully conduct a sprint-based Agile Audit:

Commitment from the client: Delivering in short sprints typically requires the client to commit to less of their own work to accommodate the investment of their time with the auditors. Delivering over a longer time period spreads that investment over that longer time period, so there's less of a visible impact in the short term.

Successful sprint-based audits also require commitment from the auditors. Moving straight from the waterfall process to Agile Auditing is a radical change, so the auditors must commit to experimenting and working with a certain level of discomfort or uncertainty while learning this way of working.

Commitment from Audit Leadership is also essential. For example, when asking the auditors to swarm on a sprint-based Agile Audit, the auditors likely won't be as successful if they're also working with their normal workload, which can be a large number of other audits, especially if those audits leverage different ways of working. Shifting between these audits with different clients, subject matters, and ways of working adds unnecessary challenges, particularly in the early stages of adopting Agile Auditing. While I'm not necessarily advocating that auditors only work on one audit at a time, Internal Audit leadership should consider the need to account for a learning curve, as well as the need for more dedicated focus on a concentrated delivery timeline, and adjust workloads and assignments accordingly.

In the instances where the client, auditors, and Internal Audit leadership make these commitments, the organization can benefit greatly from performing sprint-based audits. Conversely, in instances where these three groups are not yet ready to make these commitments, it is probably best to consider another way of implementing Auditing with Agility. A single organization may have commitment from all three parties for one particular audit and not have the same level of commitment on another audit. That's why having a plethora of options, like all of the concepts outlined in this book, is a recipe for success.

Perhaps instead of going straight to sprint-based audits, auditors could choose to incorporate a single practice from each of Chapters 5, 6, and 7. Starting with relatively simple changes that auditors can implement immediately can create momentum as simple changes are less burdensome, and the value is realized sooner.

The bottom line is that blanket edicts, like exclusively using sprint-based audits in every situation, are rarely effective when adopting better ways of working. In fact, forcing a specific process onto a team is quite the opposite of agility. Said another way, imposing an edict that a specific process must be used for all audits is the antithesis of being agile. You can't claim to be an "Agile Audit shop" if you're going against the very core of agility. That's why this book provides a large variety of concepts and practices for organizations to choose from to create a customized approach best suited for each unique situation. It is intended to be revisited repeatedly as organizations continue to seek ways to increase their value. Instead of passing an edict requiring adherence to a single process to add value to the work, set clear objectives and desired outcomes (increase collaboration with the client, get value into the client's hands sooner, align more closely with top risks, etc.), offer a menu of options from which the team may choose, and empower the team to select the approach that best aligns with those objectives and outcomes, given each unique situation.

Drop the Binary Thinking

Another behavior that tends to emerge when moving to better ways of working is to start delineating audits as "Agile" or "not Agile." You'll hear questions like "How do you handle report writing (or workpaper reviews, or any other activity) when you're doing an Agile audit?" or "Will this audit be an Agile audit?" These questions reflect a mindset that agility is something you do and that it is a binary choice (Agile or not). This too can derail your efforts. With this mindset, organizations begin to measure success in ways that may incentivize the wrong behavior, thus reducing the chances of achieving the intended outcome. For example, in viewing audits as either Agile or not Agile, leaders trying to implement agility may start to track the number of Agile audits and create targets based on these metrics. An example of such a metric is targeting to have at least 50% of audits in a year to be Agile audits. This then forces the organization to define what constitutes an Agile audit, which in most cases means strictly sprint-based audits. The unintended consequence of this is that to meet the target performance metric (at least 50% of audits completed each year are Agile audits), a specific process will likely be applied to audits that may not be the best candidate for such an approach. Instead of adopting a mindset of "Agile" or "not Agile," organizations should adopt a mindset of agility, where the focus is on selecting a way of working that will support achievement of the overall objectives and intended outcomes. In auditing, that objective is to deliver value to the organization through risk assurance and insights, so auditors should adopt a mindset that empowers them to select a way of working that enables achievement of that objective.

In reality, the binary choice should be whether to stay stagnant and slowly lose the value you provide to your organization or practice better ways of working. Once you decide to improve your ways of working, the possible paths to follow are innumerable, you just need to know what outcomes you desire. If your organization has chosen to apply a sprint-based Agile Audit framework on every audit, you can still benefit from the practices in this book. While delivering in sprints, you can also incorporate features of Auditing with Agility, like integrated planning, real-time feedback loops, and increased visibility (as well as many of the other practices in Chapters 5 through 7).

As illustrated throughout this book, there are a number of innovative ways of working (or choices on the smorgasbord) to help teams make the move to delighting their stakeholders using Auditing with Agility. Some teams may choose to incorporate all of these ways of working, while others will pick and choose the concepts that make the most sense for each particular audit, creating a customized approach. Either path will yield great benefits for both the audit team and the client.

The key takeaway in this section is to apply the concepts outlined in this book to the journey itself as well. Handing down mandates to work in a specific way, beginning the journey focused first on tools, and binary thinking (Agile versus not Agile) are common pitfalls of implementing the improved ways of working outlined in this book. Fear not, as you are well equipped with the knowledge needed to overcome these challenges and enjoy the benefits of Auditing with Agility:

- Focus on people and processes, then find a tool to support your people and improved processes.
- Set clear objectives and empower the team to select the path to achieving those objectives.
- Anchor to the concepts of value-driven auditing, integrated auditing, and adaptable auditing, selecting practices from each of those areas to create a customized approach for an audit.

With this knowledge, you are well prepared to begin your journey and start realizing the benefits of better ways of working sooner and with greater consistency.

Making the Case to Audit Leadership

Armed with everything you've learned in this book, you're ready to start implementing Auditing with Agility. How do you make the case to the audit organization? Both auditors and the client play a key role in this process.

For those of you who are auditors, your leaders need to know that they absolutely must change their ways of working to stay relevant and to add value to the organization. Failure to do so will cause our profession to become a thing of the past. Norman Marks (former chief audit executive, published author, and recipient of multiple awards from the IIA) emphasized the importance of changing the audit approach in a 2021 blog post:

> If we are not prepared to change when everything around us is changing, we are doomed. Just because we have been successful in the past doesn't mean that the same practices will make us successful today and tomorrow.[11]

You can't afford to sit back and let this happen. The audit profession must change to stay relevant and help organizations achieve their objectives.

For those of you who represent the client, your input is incredibly important as well. You are one of the key stakeholders of your organization. Your auditors need to know the problems you're facing and that you have the solutions. In order for you to achieve your objectives, you can't waste time on activities that don't help you accomplish your objectives. You can't afford not to have your auditors adapt their ways of working. You can't afford for them not to adopt Auditing with Agility. If the audit profession fails to change and is "doomed," who will help you see around the corner and help you identify risks getting in your way? You need your auditors, and your auditors need your voice. Help them make the case to their leaders and other stakeholders so they evolve into the audit organization they should be . . . and need to be.

Making the Case to the Client

It's not just the auditors who need to be on board. You need to make the case to the client as well. Help them see the benefits the organization will realize with Auditing with Agility. Help them understand what's expected of them as the auditors evolve to meet the ever-changing needs of the organization. They are expected to partner with the auditors and invest time in helping them understand what's most important to the organization, including what's most important to the client and the organization's ultimate customers. Help the client see how auditors can be their secret weapon against competitors. Doing so will position the client, and ultimately the whole organization, for success.

Conclusion: A Call to Action

As you approach the end of this book, regardless of whether you read this cover to cover or if you skipped around to the sections of most interest to you based on where you are on your journey, I have a few action items for you.

The first is to share what you've learned with at least three others. You can accomplish this in a number of ways, including practicing what you've learned and explaining to others what you're doing; sharing during a team or department meeting; hosting a book club to discuss this book with your friends, colleagues, or clients; or having a conversation with your clients (or your auditors if you're an audit client) over a cup of coffee and discussing what you've learned. Sharing with others is also a way of reinforcing what you've learned and moving from the theoretical or academic phase of your journey to that of practical application. Sharing what you've learned supports a number of the concepts in this book, like feedback loops.

I also challenge you to select one practice or item in this book and experiment with it *today*. As tempting as it may be to wait until you feel 100% ready to implement these practices perfectly, don't wait. It's okay if your experiment doesn't yield the exact results you expect. What's important is that you are learning from your experiences and that you are progressing.

I encourage you to start with one practice, or just a few practices at first, and truly treat it as an experiment with the intended outcome of learning. Perhaps you will learn that the new practices are a great fit for your organization. Maybe instead, you'll learn that more upfront communication with your team would have helped drive more success. Or you may learn that you need additional support from your leaders (and you may gain clarity on what that support looks like) to progress on your journey. Regardless of what you learn, you will have indeed taken a great step forward. You will be better equipped to try again or to select another concept to experiment with (in the instance of success and learning your organization has a strong appetite and readiness for Auditing with Agility).

Finally, I ask that you not limit yourself to only the practices outlined in this book. While comprehensive, this book is not intended to be a step-by-step guide for you to implement. Instead, it presents you with a plethora of ideas and battle-tested practices to help you progress on your journey. The examples provided in this book are not intended for you to lift and shift directly to your organization. Rather, they are intended to illustrate a situation where the theory could be and has been applied, providing you with concepts you can customize to best fit your organization.

Note for clients: While many of the action items in this book are within the auditor's control, you have the unique ability to influence a better audit experience for yourself using the information in this book. There are a number of ways you can influence a better audit experience. The first is by offering to coach the auditors through the learning curve as they experiment with these better ways of working. If you or your team have experience with any of these practices, share your own experiences with your auditors and help them on their journey. Teach them to use a task board to make work visible. Demonstrate how to run effective stand-ups and retrospective reviews. Encourage experimentation and learning from failure to encourage a more innovative mindset with your auditors.

Even if you don't have experience working in these ways, support your auditors on their journey by being open to their experimentation with better ways of working. Keep an open mind. Encourage your team to work more collaboratively with the auditors and actively participate in the audit rather than passively letting it happen to them. Encourage buy-in from your teams and your leaders. Finally, share what you've learned from this book with your auditors. These are simple actions you and your team can take to influence a better relationship between you and your auditors, resulting in a more value-added (and fun!) experience during your next audit.

Appendix

Much in the same way that DevOps leverages Agile practices, and Agile built upon Lean concepts, the concepts presented in this book are rooted in Agile, Scrum, and DevOps principles and practices. Thus, I've placed more details on many of these practices and cultures here in this appendix. But I also encourage you to go out and read many of the great books around each of these ideas.

Agile

Agile software development is based on the Agile Manifesto, which is composed of four values and twelve principles. The four values are as follows:[1]

- Individuals and interactions over processes and tools
- Working software over comprehensive documentation
- Customer collaboration over contract negotiation
- Responding to change over following a plan

While three of the four of those values translate directly to audit work, one of them doesn't. Specifically, valuing working software does not. In Chapter 5, we modified that principle as follows: valuing actionable insights over extensive documentation.

In addition to the four values, the Agile Manifesto includes twelve principles to add agility to software development. The Agile Alliance defines these principles as follows:[2]

1. Our highest priority is to satisfy the customer through early and continuous delivery of valuable software.
2. Welcome changing requirements, even late in development. Agile processes harness change for the customer's competitive advantage.

3. Deliver working software frequently, from a couple of weeks to a couple of months, with a preference to the shorter timescale.

4. Business people and developers must work together daily throughout the project.

5. Build projects around motivated individuals. Give them the environment and support they need, and trust them to get the job done.

6. The most efficient and effective method of conveying information to and within a development team is face-to-face conversation.

7. Working software is the primary measure of progress.

8. Agile processes promote sustainable development. The sponsors, developers, and users should be able to maintain a constant pace indefinitely.

9. Continuous attention to technical excellence and good design enhances agility.

10. Simplicity—the art of maximizing the amount of work not done—is essential.

11. The best architectures, requirements, and designs emerge from self-organizing teams.

12. At regular intervals, the team reflects on how to become more effective, then tunes and adjusts its behavior accordingly.

While some of these Agile principles are easily transferable to audit work, not all are as clearly relatable. Just as we modified the Agile values to better align with audit work, the twelve Agile principles can also apply to the auditing process with only slight modifications. As such, the twelve principles of Auditing with Agility are as follows:

1. Satisfy stakeholders through early and continuous delivery of value.

2. Embrace changes, even late in the audit process.

3. Deliver value frequently.

4. Auditors and their clients work together daily.

5. Build projects around motivated individuals; support and empower them.

6. Prefer face-to-face conversation over asynchronous communication.

7. Delivery of value is the primary measure of progress.

8. Promote sustainable work; the team should be able to maintain a consistent pace indefinitely.

9. Pay continuous attention to technical excellence and quality work.

10. Pursue simplicity.

11. Leverage self-organizing teams.

12. Reflect on how to become more effective, and adjust behavior accordingly.

Scrum

Scrum is a framework used primarily in software development where teams work together to achieve a shared goal, typically by delivering value iteratively. Scrum teams use sprints to deliver in iterations.

Because Agile Auditing closely resembles the Scrum framework, some Agile Auditing teams structure their roles similarly to how Scrum teams do in a technology setting. Common roles include the following:

- Product owner
- Scrum master
- Developers/Scrum team members

At first glance, it may not be abundantly clear how these roles translate to the world of auditing. Some take a little more imagination than others.

Product Owner

Let's start with the product owner. The product owner is ultimately accountable for the product. In technology, the product is often an application or technology platform. In Agile Auditing, the product is value, so the product owner is whoever is ultimately accountable for delivering value to the client and other key stakeholders. This role is typically held by an audit leader (either the chief audit executive or one of their direct or indirect reports). In some organizations, the product owner may be the auditor in charge. There is no right or wrong answer to the question of who should play the role of product owner in the audit. Each audit organization has a unique structure with a unique distribution of accountability, both of which will influence determination of the product owner for an audit.

There may also be product owners for other portions of the audit process. For example, while an auditor in charge may be the product owner for a specific audit, the chief audit executive of the same organization may be the product owner for the audit plan itself. In this example, the auditor in charge is accountable for delivering value through a specific audit engagement, while the chief audit executive is accountable for delivery of the audit plan.

The product owner's key responsibilities include defining a vision of the product and determining what work is necessary to deliver the product. Product owners have decision rights over what tasks are included in the product's backlog and how those tasks are prioritized. The product owner is accountable for working with customers to define value to be delivered. In an audit context, the customers are the client and other key stakeholders. The product owner can also be responsible for helping to remove impediments to the team's work.

Scrum Master/Team Outcome Lead/Agile Leader

The Scrum master, also referred to as the team outcome lead, Agile leader, or another similar title, can be at any level in the audit organization. What's most important is that the Scrum master demonstrates a thorough understanding of Scrum or Agile Auditing concepts and possesses the ability to coach other team members on those concepts and practices. With the help of the product owner, the Scrum master also helps to remove impediments to the team's work. The Scrum master is an invaluable role, particularly when audit organizations are in the beginning stages of moving to Agile Auditing. The team will look to the Scrum master to guide them through the initial learning curve when moving to Agile Auditing practices. They will also look to the Scrum master to keep them focused during stand-ups, even as they become more and more accustomed to this way of working. The Scrum master is often a key role in the effective implementation of Agile Auditing.

Auditors serving as Scrum master for an audit may also take on some of the audit work, such as testing controls or drafting the audit report. Due to the steep learning curve and cultural shifts often needed to transition from a waterfall audit approach to Agile Auditing techniques, it is recommended that the Scrum master focus primarily (or solely) on their duties as Scrum master during early stages of the transformation. As the auditors become more well versed in these newer practices, Scrum masters may begin to take on more work not directly associated with the Scrum master role, as long as they do not lose sight of their accountabilities bestowed upon them as Scrum master.

Developers/Scrum Team Member

The concept of a product owner and a Scrum master are fairly easy to grasp when transferring from a technology-focused application to application in the audit process. The role of developer does not immediately translate as clearly. Developers in a technology organization are accountable for developing the features or the elements that will culminate into the final product. They're the ones doing the hands-on work that goes into delivering the product. In an Agile Audit, the "developers" are the individual auditors who are accountable for completing the work necessary to deliver value to the client, and are sometimes called "Scrum team members." These are typically the staff assigned to the audit, who are accountable primarily for testing controls and articulating audit observations.

A key concept related to teams under the Agile Audit methodology is that the team must collectively possess the skills necessary to accomplish tasks to achieve the team's goal. Translating this to the world of auditing, an Agile Audit team needs to have the skills necessary to conduct the audit. Each team member need not individually possess all of those skills; rather, each team member should bring a skill or skills, such that when combined, the team has the skills it needs to effectively perform the audit work.

Estimating Story Points

In Chapter 5, you learned about the practice of increasing the visibility of work. Teams that make their work visible often estimate the effort needed to complete work. Story points are another way of describing the amount of time or work it takes to complete a task. There are a few different ways you can estimate story points, including Fibonacci numbers and T-shirt sizes. I outline a few options below.

The Fibonacci numbers are a sequence of numbers, where the next number in the sequence is the sum of the two preceding numbers (1, 1, 2, 3, 5, 8, 13 . . .). Using these numbers to estimate effort for audit tasks might look something like this:

- 1 point: Straightforward tasks requiring minimal effort to complete (e.g., scheduling a meeting with another individual or completing a fifteen-minute training course)
- 2 points: Fairly straightforward tasks requiring a small level of effort (e.g., scheduling a meeting with a large audience or completing a thirty-minute training course)
- 3 points: A slightly more complex task requiring a medium level of effort (e.g., documenting the risk and control matrix, testing the design of a control or testing the operating effectiveness of a control with a small sample size)
- 5 points: A more complex task requiring a large level of effort (e.g., testing both the design and operating effectiveness of a control with a small sample size)
- 8 points: A complex task requiring an extremely large level of effort (e.g., testing or an entire population or a large sample, building a test using data analytics, an all-day training)

Using T-shirt sizes as a method of estimating points may appeal more to those who prefer visualization:

- XS: Straightforward tasks requiring minimal effort to complete
- Small: Fairly straightforward tasks requiring a small level of effort
- Medium: A slightly more complex task requiring a medium level of effort
- Large: A more complex task requiring a large level of effort
- XL: A complex task requiring an extremely large level of effort

Bibliography

Agile Alliance. "What is Agile?" AgileAlliance.org. Accessed November 7, 2022. https://www.agilealliance.org/agile101/.

Beck, Kent, et al. "The 12 Principles behind the Agile Manifesto." AgileAlliance.org. Accessed November 7, 2022. https://www.agilealliance.org/agile101/12-prin ciples-behind-the-agile-manifesto/.

Beck, Kent, et al. "The Agile Manifesto." AgileAlliance.org. Accessed November 7, 2022. https://www.agilealliance.org/agile101/the-agile-manifesto/.

Chai, Wesley. "The Three Ways." TechTarget. Accessed November 8, 2022. https://www.techtarget.com/whatis/definition/The-Three-Ways.

Deloitte. *Agile Internal Audit Four Years On: Better, Faster, Happier? A Retrospective.* Deloitte Development LLC, 2021. https://www2.deloitte.com/content/dam /Deloitte/global/Documents/Risk/gx-agile-internal-audit-four-years.pdf.

Deloitte. *Becoming Agile: A Guide to Elevating Internal Audit's Performance and Value.* Deloitte Development LLC, 2017. https://www2.deloitte.com/content/dam /Deloitte/global/Documents/Finance/gx-fa-agile-internal-audit-introduction -elevating-performance.pdf.

Fortune. "Fortune 100 Best Companies to Work For: Capital One Financial." *Fortune.* Updated August 3, 2022. Accessed November 5, 2022. https://fortune .com/company/capital-one-financial/best-companies/.

Gagné, Chris. "Wastes Caused by Context Switching." LinkedIn.com. July 27, 2021. https://www.linkedin.com/pulse/wastes-caused-context-switching-chris -gagn%C3%A9/.

Gallup. "Employee Engagement Solutions." Gallup.com. Accessed November 7, 2022. https://www.gallup.com/workplace/229424/employee-engagement.aspx.

Gallup. "Gallup's Employee Engagement Survey: Ask the Right Questions with the Q12 Survey." Gallup.com. Accessed November 7, 2022. https://www.gallup .com/workplace/356063/gallup-q12-employee-engagement-survey.aspx.

Ganann, Laura. "Beyond Agile: Walmart's Journey to Value-Driven & Customer-Centric Auditing." Auditboard.com. December 19, 2019. https://www.audit board.com/blog/beyond-agile-auditing-walmarts-journey/.

Gartner, *Flattening the Hierarchy: How Reaology's Audit Team Went Full Agile*. Gartner, May 2022.

Harvard University Risk Management & Audit Services. *How long will my audit take?* RMAS.FAD.Hardvard.edu. Accessed November 5, 2022. https://rmas. fad.harvard.edu/faq/how-long-will-my-audit-take.

Institute of Internal Auditors. *2018 North American Pulse of Internal Audit*. Lake Mary, FL: The Institute of Internal Auditors, 2018. https://www.theiia.org /globalassets/site/content/articles/industry-knowledge-brief/2018/2018 -na-pulse-of-internal-audit-financial-services-focus/2018-north-american -pulse-of-internal-audit-financial-focus.pdf.

Institute of Internal Auditors. "About Internal Audit." TheIIA.org, accessed November 1, 2022, https://www.theiia.org/en/about-us/about-internal-audit/.

Institute of Internal Auditors. *Agile Auditing: Sprinting to Change: Reimagining Internal Audit in a Digital World*. Lake Mary, FL: The Institute of Internal Auditors, 2018. https://www.theiia.org/globalassets/site/content/articles /industry-knowledge-brief/2018/agile-auditing/iia-fs-agile-auditing.pdf.

Institute of Internal Auditors. *Agile Internal Audit: Leading Practices on the Journey to Becoming Agile*. Lake Mary, FL: The Institute of Internal Auditors, 20TK.

Institute of Internal Auditors. "Attribute Standards." TheIIA.org. Accessed November 7, 2022. https://www.theiia.org/en/standards/what-are-the-standards /mandatory-guidance/standards/attribute-standards/.

Institute of Internal Auditors. *Continuing Professional Education Policy: Requirements for Certification & Qualification*. Lake Mary, FL: The Institute of Internal Auditors, 2022. https://www.theiia.org/globalassets/documents/certifications /cpe-policy.pdf.

Institute of Internal Auditors. *The IIA's Three Lines Model: An Update of the Three Lines of Defense*. Lake Mary, FL: The Institute of Internal Auditors, 2020. https://www.theiia.org/globalassets/documents/resources/the-iias-three -lines-model-an-update-of-the-three-lines-of-defense-july-2020/three -lines-model-updated-english.pdf.

Institute of Internal Auditors. Implementation Guides. Lake Mary, FL: The Institute of Internal Auditors, 2016. https://www.theiia.org/globalassets /documents/standards/implementation-guides-gated/2017-implementation -guides-all.pdf.

Institute of Internal Auditors. *Integrated Auditing*. Lake Mary, FL: The Institute of Internal Auditors, 2012. https://www.theiia.org/globalassets/documents

/content/articles/guidance/practice-guides/integrated-auditing/pg-integrated
-auditing.pdf.

Institute of Internal Auditors. *Internal Auditing: Assurance, Insight, and Objectivity*. Lake Mary, FL: The Institute of Internal Auditors, 20XX. https://www
.theiia.org/globalassets/documents/about-us/what-is-internal-audit/ia
-assurance-insight-and-objectivity.pdf.

Institute of Internal Auditors. "Mission of Internal Audit." TheIIA.org. Accessed
August 28, 2022 https://www.theiia.org/en/standards/mission-of-internal
-audit/.

Institute of Internal Auditors. *Official IIA Glossary*. The Institute of Internal Auditors: November 1, 2020. https://www.theiia.org/globalassets/documents
/certifications/the-iia-official-glossary/official-iia-glossary-english.pdf.

Institute of Internal Auditors. "Performance Standards." TheIIA.org. Accessed
November 7, 2022. https://www.theiia.org/en/standards/what-are-the
-standards/mandatory-guidance/standards/performance-standards/.

ISACA. *Continuing Professional Education (CPE) Policy*. Rolling Meadows, IL: ISACA,
2014. https://www.isaca.org/-/media/files/isacadp/project/isaca/certification
/cisa/cisa-cpe/cisa-cpe-english.pdf.

ISACA. Destination: Agile Auditing. Schaumburg, IL: ISACA, 2021.

ITAuditSecurity. "Why Hate Auditors?" ITauditSecurity. January 13, 2010. https://
itauditsecurity.wordpress.com/2010/01/13/why-hate-auditors/.

Lindow, Paul E., and Jill D. Race. "Beyond Traditional Audit Techniques." *Journal
of Accountancy*. June 30, 2002. https://www.journalofaccountancy.com
/issues/2002/jul/beyondtraditionalaudittechniques.html.

Kim, Gene. "The Three Ways: The Principles Underpinning DevOps."
ITRevolution.com. August 22, 2012. https://itrevolution.com/articles/the
-three-ways-principles-underpinning-devops/.

Kim, Gene, Jez Humble, Patrick Debois, John Willis, and Nicole Forsgren, PhD.
*The DevOps Handbook: How to Create World-Class Agility, Reliability, & Secu-
rity in Technology Organizations*, Second Edition. Portland, OR: IT Revolution,
2020.

Kristensen, Ida, Merlina Manocaran, Edmond Sannini, and Haris Usman. "Building
the Internal-Audit Function of the Future." McKinsey & Company. Febru-
ary 18, 2021. https://www.mckinsey.com/capabilities/risk-and-resilience
/our-insights/building-the-internal-audit-function-of-the-future.

Mark, Gloria. "Too Many Interruptions at Work?" Interview by Jennifer Robison.
Gallup.com. June 8, 2006. https://news.gallup.com/businessjournal/23146
/too-many-interruptions-work.aspx.

Marks, Norman. "8 Biggest Risks for Internal Auditors in 2018." CMS Wire. November 17, 2017. https://www.cmswire.com/information-management /8-biggest-risks-for-internal-auditors-in-2018/.

Marks, Norman. *Auditing That Matters*. 2016.

Marks, Norman. "8 Biggest Risks for Internal Auditors in 2018." CMS Wire. November 17, 2017. https://www.cmswire.com/information-management /8-biggest-risks-for-internal-auditors-in-2018/.

Marks, Norman. "Is Agile Auditing the Latest Fad or a Really Great Practice?" Norman Marks's blog. April 30, 2021. https://normanmarks.wordpress .com/2021/04/30/is-agile-auditing-the-latest-fad-or-a-really-great-practice/.

Oyler, Stephanie. "How Long Does it Take to Complete a SOC 2 Audit?" Cloud Security Alliance blog. September 15, 2022. https://cloudsecurityalliance.org /blog/2022/09/15/how-long-does-it-take-to-complete-a-soc-2-audit/.

Protiviti. "Capital One: Transforming Digitally and Operationally to Become an 'Industry Beacon.'" Protiviti (Volume 15). Accessed November 7, 2022. https://www.protiviti.com/US-en/insights/iaworld-capital-one.

Pugliese, Anthony. "CEO Message: The Nature of Innovation." *Internal Auditor* (June 2022). https://internalauditor.theiia.org/en/articles/2022/june/the -nature-of-innovation/.

PwC. *Agile Auditing: Mindset over Matter*. PriceWaterhouseCoopers LLP, 2018. https://www.pwc.co.uk/audit-assurance/assets/pdf/agile-auditing.pdf.

PwC. *Avoiding Change Is Not an Option: Why the Time to Transform Internal Audit Is Now*. PriceWaterhouseCoopers LLP: 2020. https://www.pwc.com/us/en /services/risk-assurance/assets/pwc-transform-internal-audit-avoiding -change-is-not-an-option.pdf.

Smart, Jonathan, Zsolt Berend, Myles Ogilvie, and Simon Rohrer. *Sooner Safer Happier: Antipatterns and Patterns for Business Agility*. Portland, OR: IT Revolution, 2020.

TeamMate. "The 7 Habits of Highly Ineffective Auditors." WoltersKluwer.com. August 17, 2018. https://www.wolterskluwer.com/en/expert-insights/the -7-habits-of-highly-ineffective-auditors.

The University of Texas at Austin Office of Internal Audits. "Audit Process." UTexas.edu. Accessed on November 5, 2022. https://audit.utexas.edu/ audit-process.

"Velocity 09: John Allspaw and Paul Hammond, '10+ Deploys Per Day.'," Posted by O'Reilly, posted on June 25, 2009. YouTube video, 46:21. https://www.you tube.com/watch?v=LdOe18KhtT4.

Weatherspoon, Zack, and Richard Chambers. "Zack Weatherspoon of John Deere Champions a Consultative Approach That Drives Value." Auditboard.com. September 2, 2022. https://www.auditboard.com/blog/agents-of-change -zack-weatherspoon-of-john-deere//

Weingerb, Gerald M. *Quality Software Management: Systems Thinking.* Dorset House: New York, 1992.

Wright, Aaron. "What is Agile Auditing? The Benefits of Taking Your Audit Team Agile." Auditboard. September 30, 2020. https://www.auditboard.com/blog/ what-is-agile-auditing-benefits/.

Notes

Introduction

1. Kim et al., *The DevOps Handbook*, xxv.
2. Kim et al., *The DevOps Handbook*, xxv.

Chapter 1

1. Institute of Internal Auditors, "About Internal Audit," TheIIA.org.
2. Institute of Internal Auditors, "Mission of Internal Audit," TheIIA.org.
3. Institute of Internal Auditors, "Internal Auditing," 3.
4. Institute of Internal Auditors, *The IIA's Three Lines Model*.
5. Institute of Internal Auditors, "Mission of Internal Audit," TheIIA.org.
6. The University of Texas at Austin Office of Internal Audits, "Audit Process"; Harvard University Risk Management & Audit Services, *How long will my audit take?*; Oyler, "How Long Does it Take to Complete a SOC 2 Audit?"
7. PwC, *Avoiding Change Is Not an Option*.
8. PwC, *Avoiding Change Is Not an Option*.
9. PwC, *Avoiding Change Is Not an Option*.
10. Kristensen, Manocaran, Sannini, and Usman, "Building the Internal-Audit Function of the Future."
11. Smart, Berend, Ogilvie, and Rohrer, *Sooner Safer Happier*, 223.
12. Smart, Berend, Ogilvie, and Rohrer, *Sooner Safer Happier*, 223.
13. Fortune, "Fortune 100 Best Companies to Work For: Capital One Financial."
14. Institute of Internal Auditors, *Agile Auditing: Sprinting to Change*.
15. Institute of Internal Auditors, *Agile Auditing: Sprinting to Change*.
16. Lindow and Race, "Beyond Traditional Audit Techniques."
17. TeamMate, "The 7 Habits of Highly Ineffective Auditors."
18. TeamMate, "The 7 Habits of Highly Ineffective Auditors."
19. ITAuditSecurity, "Why Hate Auditors?"

20. Marks, "8 Biggest Risks for Internal Auditors in 2018."

21. Marks, "8 Biggest Risks for Internal Auditors in 2018."

22. Marks, "8 Biggest Risks for Internal Auditors in 2018."

23. Marks, "8 Biggest Risks for Internal Auditors in 2018."

24. Marks, "8 Biggest Risks for Internal Auditors in 2018."

Chapter 2

1. Institute of Internal Auditors, *2018 North American Pulse of Internal Audit.*

2. Institute of Internal Auditors, *2018 North American Pulse of Internal Audit.*

3. Agile Alliance, "What Is Agile?"

4. Institute of Internal Auditors, *Agile Auditing: Sprinting to Change.*

5. Deloitte, *Becoming Agile.*

6. PWC, *Agile Auditing: Mindset over Matter.*

7. Becca Kinney and Dan Greenfield, interview with the author, September 2, 2022.

8. Gartner, *Flattening the Hierarchy.*

9. Institute of Internal Auditors, *Agile Internal Audit: Leading Practices on the Journey to Becoming Agile.*

10. Becca Kinney and Dan Greenfield, interview with the author, September 2, 2022.

11. Becca Kinney and Dan Greenfield, interview with the author, September 2, 2022.

12. ISACA. *Destination: Agile Auditing.*

13. ISACA. *Destination: Agile Auditing.*

14. Institute of Internal Auditors, *2018 North American Pulse of Internal Audit.*

15. Wright, "What is Agile Auditing?"

16. Deloitte, *Agile Internal Audit Four Years On.*

17. Deloitte, *Agile Internal Audit Four Years On.*

18. Deloitte, *Agile Internal Audit Four Years On.*

19. "Velocity 09: John Allspaw and Paul Hammond, '10+ Deploys Per Day,'" YouTube video.

20. Chai, "The Three Ways."

21. Kim, "The Three Ways: The Principles Underpinning DevOps."

22. Kim et al., *The DevOps Handbook*, 3.

23. Kim, "The Three Ways: The Principles Underpinning DevOps."

24. Kim et al., *The DevOps Handbook*, 37 & 287.

Chapter 3

1. Personal communication with the author, 2022.
2. "Velocity 09: John Allspaw and Paul Hammond, '10+ Deploys Per Day,'" YouTube video.
3. Institute of Internal Auditors, *Integrated Auditing*.
4. Ganann, "Beyond Agile: Walmart's Journey to Value-Driven & Customer-Centric Auditing."
5. Gallup, "Employee Engagement Solutions."
6. Gallup, "Gallup's Employee Engagement Survey."

Chapter 4

1. Weinberg, *Quality Software Management*, 284.
2. Mark, "Too Many Interruptions at Work?"
3. Smart, Berend, Ogilvie, and Rohrer, *Sooner Safer Happier*, 111.
4. Institute of Internal Auditors, *Official IIA Glossary*.

Chapter 5

1. Marks, *Auditing that Matters*, 45–50.
2. Weatherspoon and Chambers, "Zack Weatherspoon of John Deere Champions Consultative Approach That Drives Value."
3. Institute of Internal Auditors, "Performance Standards."
4. Institute of Internal Auditors, "Performance Standards."
5. Institute of Internal Auditors, "About Internal Audit," TheIIA.org.
6. Institute of Internal Auditors, "Performance Standards."

Chapter 6

1. Becca Kinney and Dan Greenfield, interview with the author, September 2, 2022.
2. Kim et al., *The DevOps Handbook*, 3.
3. Kim et al., *The DevOps Handbook*, 27.
4. Institute of Internal Auditors, "Performance Standards."

Chapter 7

1. Becca Kinney and Dan Greenfield, interview with the author, September 2, 2022.
2. Institute of Internal Auditors, "Attribute Standards."
3. Institute of Internal Auditors, *Implementation Guides*, 38.
4. Institute of Internal Auditors, "Performance Standards."

Chapter 8

1. Pugliese, "CEO Message: The Nature of Innovation," 8.
2. Institute of Internal Auditors, "Attribute Standards."
3. Institute of Internal Auditors, *Continuing Professional Education Policy*.
4. ISACA, *Continuing Professional Education (CPE) Policy*.
5. Anywhere Real Estate, personal interview with the author, September 9, 2022.
6. Sally Clark, email correspondence with the author, December 11, 2022.
7. Protiviti, "Capital One: Transforming Digitally and Operationally to Become an 'Industry Beacon.'"
8. Steve Murdock, personal interview with the author, September 12, 2022.

Chapter 9

1. Institute of Internal Auditors, *2018 North American Pulse of Internal Audit*.
2. Institute of Internal Auditors, "About Internal Audit," TheIIA.org.
3. Institute of Internal Auditors, "Attribute Standards."
4. Institute of Internal Auditors, *The IIA's Three Lines Model*.
5. Institute of Internal Auditors, "Performance Standards."
6. Institute of Internal Auditors, "Performance Standards."
7. Institute of Internal Auditors, "Performance Standards."
8. Institute of Internal Auditors, "Performance Standards."
9. Institute of Internal Auditors, "Performance Standards."
10. Institute of Internal Auditors, "About Internal Audit," TheIIA.org.
11. Marks, "Is Agile Auditing the Latest Fad or a Really Great Practice?"

Appendix

1. Beck, et al., "The Agile Manifesto."
2. Beck, et al., "The 12 Principles behind the Agile Manifesto."

Acknowledgments

As is a theme carried throughout this book, the best work is done not in isolation but with high levels of collaboration and support. The process of writing this book has been spot-on consistent with that theme. This book would not be where it is today if not for the support and contributions of others. While there are too many individual names to list, a few are listed below. To those who are not specifically called out here, your contributions and support are not unnoticed or unappreciated. I appreciate you more than you know.

First and foremost, I want to thank my family. Christian, thank you for believing in me and for being my inspiration to keep going. Chris, thank you for supporting me by creating space for me to take on this enormous challenge and continuously providing words of encouragement to combat my self-doubt. Thank you to my parents, Dave and Linda Mirkovich, for your unwavering support. To my brother, Brad Mirkovich, thank you for handing me the first book I read on Agility. To my sister, Vanessa Herreid, and the rest of my family, thank you for all of your support and love.

This book also would not have been possible without the support of my closest friends. Thank you Amanda Chaplin and Jason Rager for providing support and effective challenge, both throughout this process and for life in general. Thank you for being there to celebrate the peaks and help me through the valleys of this adventure and for believing in me even when my self-confidence wavered. Thank you to my other close friends for being in my corner as well.

Special thanks to my work family, which includes (rightfully so) auditors and audit clients. While there are far too many impactful people to call out individually, I do want to specifically thank my direct leaders, Pat Shanahan and Greg Jordan, for creating and maintaining a safe environment for and empowering me to experiment with better ways of working. Thank you to my team and my clients for humoring me and having patience as we figured this all out—from taking those first few uncertain steps on this journey to sharing knowledge, teaching each other, and providing actionable feedback along the way. None of this would have been possible without you.

Thank you to everyone on the IT Revolution team who helped me so much on this journey. Special thanks to Leah Brown for answering my seemingly endless questions, keeping me on target with key milestones and due dates, providing a fresh and thought-provoking perspective (you would make a GREAT auditor), and continuing to encourage me and keep me highly engaged on this journey. Thank you as well to Anna Noak and Alex Broderick-Forster for the impromptu Zoom calls to answer questions. And to Gene Kim for seeing what I didn't at first—that this was the start of something incredible, something to change the way we all experience audits—and for giving me the stage (literally and figuratively) to share knowledge and experiences with others to help them in their own journey.

This book has been made so much better through contributions from peer reviewers, early readers, and case study participants. Thank you to peer reviewers Tod Bickley, Jason Rager, Jon Smart, Misty Kuamoo, Yuliya Volodin, Topo Pal, and Norman Marks. The fresh perspective you provided during your review made this book so much better. Thank you to case study participants Becca Kinney, Dan Greenfield, Steve Murdock, and Sally Clark. Thank you for sharing your own journeys and contributing to the advancement of the auditing profession. Thank you to early readers Ray Ryjewski, Yosef Levine, Mike Pisano, Dr. Rainer Lenz, and Pam Pesta.

Finally, thank you to my readers. Thank you for reading this book and for your interest in improving the audit experience. This book is for you.

For all those listed above and those who I didn't list out here, I offer a sincere thank you. This truly has been an incredible experience that has brought me so much joy. It absolutely wouldn't have been possible without each and every one of you.

About the Author

Born in Pittsburgh, Pennsylvania, Clarissa Lucas is an experienced audit and risk management leader in the financial services industry. She began her writing endeavors in 2019 when she published her first white paper as part of a department learning initiative for the Fortune 100 company for which she worked. Since then she has become a thought leader for the auditing profession and began pioneering the term "Auditing with Agility" within her own team and with other local audit teams. She has written articles on Auditing with Agility that have been published by the IIA and IT Revolution. Clarissa has spoken at a number of industry conferences on this topic locally and internationally. She wants to help even more people understand this topic, so this book transpired. She hopes you use it as a tool to share and expand your own organization's influence and value-potential.

Clarissa earned her bachelor's degree in mathematics with a minor in accounting from Washington and Jefferson College and an MBA from Waynesburg University. She is a Certified Internal Auditor, Certified Information Systems Auditor, and Certified Investments and Derivatives Auditor.

She currently resides in Johnstown, Ohio, with her husband, Chris, their son, Christian, and doodle puppy, Rosie. Outside of work, Clarissa spends most of her moments with her family, reading, working out, and taking an occasional extra trip with her bestie. She can oftentimes be found in ice rinks around the Midwest, holding a hot beverage and watching her son play hockey.

DISCOVER MORE TITLES FROM
IT REVOLUTION

Helping Technology Leaders Succeed for 10 Years

Discover books, resources, and more at ITRevolution.com